S0-BZQ-638

STUDIES IN THE SYNTAX OF
BEN JONSON'S PLAYS

By the same Author

THE ACCIDENCE OF BEN JONSON'S PLAYS, MASQUES AND
ENTERTAINMENTS

THE PROBLEM OF *HENRY VIII* RE-OPENED: SOME LINGUISTIC CRITERIA
FOR THE TWO STYLES APPARENT IN THE PLAY

Studies in the Syntax
of
Ben Jonson's Plays

A. C. PARTRIDGE

Senior Lecturer in English at the University of Pretoria
Dominion Fellow, St. John's College, Cambridge
Leverhulme Research Fellow

BOWES & BOWES
CAMBRIDGE

First published in 1953 by
Bowes & Bowes Publishers Limited, Cambridge

Printed in Great Britain in the City of Oxford
at the Alden Press

CONTENTS

v

THE DEFINITE ARTICLE 88

PREFACE

In presenting these notes on Ben Jonson's syntax, I wish to record my indebtedness to Professor W. S. Mackie, Head of the Department of English at the University of Cape Town, for his encouragement and advice. Suggestions too numerous to mention I owe to him. It was his idea that I should undertake a syntax of Jonson's plays as a parallel study to the syntax of Shakespeare's, on the lines indicated in W. Franz's *Shakespeare-Grammatik*. Opportunity may offer to undertake other parts of speech at a later date. The present instalment deals with the periphrastic auxiliary verb *do*, the nouns, pronouns (excluding a treatment of the use of *thou* and *you*), and the definite article.

Syntax deals with sentence-structure, and has three main branches:

(1) The grammatical functions of parts of speech and their modified forms;

(2) Word order;

(3) Sentence formation, with particular reference to the relationship of phrases and clauses within the sentence.

In this study my main concern is with the first of these, though the third is sometimes incidentally treated. Word order has rarely been dealt with, as the greater proportion of Jonson's dramatic work is in verse, and considerations of poetic licence would only have involved me in unprofitable speculations.

It is probable that in Jonson, more than in any contemporary dramatist, we have the pattern of Elizabethan and Jacobean English as it was actually spoken. In the Prologue to *Every Man in His Humour* (Folio version) he pleads for

> . . . deedes, and language, such as men doe use:
> And persons, such as Comoedie would chuse,
> When she would shew an Image of the times,
> And sport with humane follies, not with crimes.

Whatever Jonson wrote was realistic and critical. The dialogue, especially of the earlier comedies, is an imitation of what Jonson heard in his daily contact with men and women of all classes.

Jonson's literary prose, as exemplified in the dedications of certain plays, is Latinized in its arrangement. The prose dialogue of the plays is, on the other hand, difficult to assess, being often a deliberate burlesque of some despised affectation. It was Tennyson, I believe, who spoke of Jonson in *Cynthia's Revels* as "sailing in a sea of glue". The turgid satire of court fopperies and intellectual posturing is not, however, without its interest to the student of linguistic fads and fashions. *Every Man out of His Humour* is equally weighted with documentary matter. In censuring the cant and folly of pretentious speech Jonson is topical to the point of obscurity; the purity of his comic art is seen in *The Silent Woman* and *Bartholomew Fair*.

But it is most frequently in the stricter discipline of verse drama that Jonson emerges as a virtuoso of dramatic form and a master of pellucid English. The technical accommodation of the verse to the natural forms of speech is remarkable, not only at the height of his powers in *Volpone* and *The Alchemist*, but even in the later plays such as *The New Inn* and *The Magnetic Lady*.

The importance of syntax as the basis of style has often been overlooked. English has always been more conservative in syntax than in phonology and accidence; and Jonson is probably more conservative, from the syntactical point of view, than Shakespeare. Jonson was himself a grammarian—a fact which probably makes for conservatism. But on the whole there is considerable resemblance in the grammatical use which each of these great dramatists made of the language.

The text of the plays used in citation is that made available by Herford and Simpson in the first seven volumes of their edition of Ben Jonson's works. It is an excellent critical text, and makes research a good deal more reliable than it might otherwise have been. In this edition the plays appear in chronological order, not the order of publication. I have maintained this order in the citation of references. A few interesting examples have been recorded from the masques and entertainments (Vol. VII).

The bibliography which ends these pages is far from complete. I have refrained from a long enumeration of references to periodicals. One debt, however, must be here discharged, namely, my obligation to the editors of the *New Oxford English Dictionary*.

No research of this kind is possible without constant reference to its vast stores of material.

The first section of this study appeared under the title "The Periphrastic Auxiliary Verb 'Do' and its Use in the Plays of Ben Jonson" in *The Modern Language Review* of January, 1948, and I wish to acknowledge the Editor's courtesy in allowing me to reprint it here.

My thanks are also due to the Publications Committee of the University of Pretoria for generous help in making the publication of these notes possible.

CHRONOLOGICAL LIST OF PLAYS AND ABBREVIATIONS USED

Abbreviation	Title	Written	Acted	First Published	Remarks
T.T.	A Tale of a Tub	c 1596 or 1597	1633	F₂—1640	F₂ sole authority
C.A.	The Case is Altered	c 1597 or 1598	before 1609	Q —1609	Reprinted 1756 only
E.M.I.H.	Everyman in his Humour (Italian Version)	1598	1598	Q —1601	
„ (F)	„ (English Version)			F₁—1616	Revised from Q 1601
E.M.O.H.	Every Man out of his Humour	1599	1599	Q —1600	
Revels	Cynthia's Revels	1600	1600	Q —1601	F₁ an expansion of Q
Poet.	Poetaster		1601	Q —1602	F₁ revision of Q
Sej.	Sejanus		1603	Q —1606	„ „ „
Volp.	Volpone		1605	Q —1607	„ „ „
Epic.	Epicœne or The Silent Woman		1609	Q —1612 ?	
Alch.	The Alchemist		1610	Q —1612	F₁ slightly changed Q
Cat.	Catiline		1610	Q —1611	F₁ revision of Q
Bart. F.	Bartholomew Fair		1614	F₂—1631	One of 3 plays d/d 1631 in F₂ (1640)
D.A.	The Devil is an Ass		1616	F₂—1631	„ „ „
Stap. N.	The Staple of News		1625	F₂—1631	„ „ „
N. Inn	The New Inn		1629	Oct. 1631	Reprinted F₃ (1692)
Mag. La.	The Magnetic Lady		1632	F₂—1640	
S.S.	The Sad Shepherd			F₂—1640	Title-page d/d 1641
M.F.	Mortimer his Fall			F₂—1640	Argument and two scenes

F₁ = Folio 1616—includes plays from E.M.I.H. to *Catiline*.

F₂ = Folio 1631-40 includes plays of F₁ + T.T., Bart. F.—M.F. (except N. Inn)

F₃ = Folio 1692

The figures in parentheses at the end of each citation indicate the page in the Herford and Simpson edition.

In this edition the First Folio, which was carefully corrected by Jonson, is the authority for all the plays it contains, i.e. up to and including *Catiline*.

I

1. THE PERIPHRASTIC AUXILIARY VERB 'DO'

1. The origin and use of the periphrastic auxiliary verb 'do'

Various analyses of the modern usage are available, the most orderly being that of the *N.E.D.* For the Elizabethan practice I have found Franz's "Die Umschreibung mit 'do' in Shakespeare's Prosa" (*Eng. Studien*, vol. 54, p. 297) the most useful. For the historical evolution I am indebted to Langenfelt's *Select Studies in Colloquial English of the late Middle Ages* (pp. 98-129), Jesperson's *Growth and Structure of the English Language* (ch. VIII, § 211), Bradley's *Making of English* (p. 70), Sweet's *New English Grammar* (vol. II, pp. 87-92), and Engblom's *On the Origin and Early Development of the Auxiliary Do*.

The O.E. examples given in the *N.E.D.* under *do* as a periphrastic auxiliary (25a and b) are

c 893 K. Alfred *Oros.* i. x. § 5 Æftre ðæm hīe *dydon* æʒþer ʒe cyninga rīcu settan ʒe nīwu ceastra timbredon.

c 888 K. Alfred *Boeth.* VI. Swā *dōþ* nū þā þeostro þīnre ʒedrēfednesse wiþstandan mīnum leohtum lārum.

Both these appear to be causative uses; and it is probable that the periphrastic auxiliary developed from this source in Middle English.[1] Langenfelt says that the causative sense was gradually lost owing to the outward appearance of nouns and verbs from the same stem often being identical in this period. 'Why *do* ye wepe?' occurs in Chaucer's *Monk's Tale* (c 1386); but the use of periphrastic *do* seems to have been rare in literary works before 1400.[2] Langenfelt thinks Chaucer's instance was introduced for the purpose of "local colour", the speaker being a child.

If early writers were conservative in their avoidance of periphrastic *do*, in the spoken language it may have been quite common.

---

[1] There is an interesting example, still causative, in Michael of Northgate's *Ayenbyte of Inwyt* (mid. 14th C) Þise uorbisne sseweþ wel þet merci is guod chapuare, vor hi deþ wexe þe timliche guodes.

[2] Engblom (*On the Origin and Early Development of the Auxiliary Do*, p. 37) has found a negative example in the *Early South-English Legendary* (c. 1280): ʒwane we In godes serviše beoth: we ne doʒ nouʒt ore ordre *breke*.

The use of the preterite *gan*, an aphetic form of *began*, in M.E. verse is sometimes quoted as a parallel instance of periphrasis (for instance by the *N.E.D.*); but if the function of *gan* in *he gan wepe* was temporal, the meaning of the sentence was not the same as *he wept*.

What is unaccounted for historically is the development of emphatic *do*. Engblom attempts, with some plausibility, to show that emphatic *do* is derived from the pro-verb or substitute *do*, and that it is only the unemphatic uses that are derived from the causative.

In the 15th and 16th centuries literary writers with a taste for elegance in style continued to avoid periphrasis with *do*. Lydgate was the first to cultivate it extensively, but he used it mainly in positive sentences.

It is convenient to consider the positional usage of *not* with this periphrasis, as the history of the two overlaps. The negative adverb (or particle) *ne* was located in O.E. before the verb, and this was the origin of the frequent Elizabethan verse order *I not saw*. But *not* itself is derived from the O.E. indef. pronoun *noht*,[1] not from the adverb *ne*. Its other Elizabethan position e.g. *I saw not*, the usual order for dignified language, is a survival of the frequent use of double negatives. For it was natural in such sentences as *I ne saw not* that the unstressed *ne* should cease to be used. *Ne* preceding (and in combination with) the verb survives only in *willy nilly*; *not* after the main verb is preserved, somewhat archaically, in a few conventional expressions like *I know not, I care not, I doubt not, I mistake not*.

The object of affirmative periphrasis, Jesperson holds, was to keep the normal order of the subject before the notional verb when a desire for emphasis tended to disturb it. This we see achieved, for instance, in the N.E. form of questions, e.g. '*Do you think so ?*', which replaced the common Elizabethan '*Think you so ?*'. Similarly, the evolution of negative periphrasis is accounted for by a tendency in Indo-Germanic languages to place the negative adverb before the notional verb. Thus in the sentence *I do not think so*, both the subject *I* and the negative *not* are placed before the notional verb *think*, while *do*, which

---

[1] This persisted plainly in such sentences as the following, now out of date, but not uncommon in 16th C:—
Bart. F. I. 3. 146 (27) ha' *not* to doe with him.

4

gives the all-important person, number and tense of the compound verb, follows immediately after its subject. Unfortunately *not* is now placed in the unemphatic middle position and so becomes weakened in conversation and combined with the preceding auxiliary, as in the colloquial *I don't think so.*

By the beginning of the 16th C the use of periphrasis had become so common and so undiscriminating in its grammatical and emphatic function that it was everywhere synonymous with the simple present or past indicative. It is still so employed in the S.W. dialects of England and occasionally in modern verse for the sake of metre. This loose usage fell justly out of favour about the middle of the 18th C, when periphrastic *do* was standardized in its modern emphatic, interrogative and negative functions. It then came to be used in simple affirmative statements only after certain conjunctive adverbs, as in the sentence *So gracefully does he dance.* If analysed, all the uses of modern Standard English have a slightly emphatic significance, *do* only being used when it is desirable to split the verb into two parts, and to place the stress on the auxiliary. Word order is that of the other auxiliaries *shall, will* and *have* in the future and perfect tenses. The periphrastic use of *do* is now confined to the present and past indicative and imperative. In its earlier history it was also used with the infinitive and past participle.

To give an adequate historical survey of the subject, with special reference to Jonson's practice, I have found it necessary to include many non-periphrastic alternatives which were in use in the 16th C. The arrangement is self-explanatory.

A. INDICATIVE

I. AFFIRMATIVE

(a) Statements

Franz's subdivisions (*Shakespeare-Grammatik*, § 595), viz. emphasis, intensification and actuality, are difficult to justify. The following arrangement is more convenient ; but it must be added that the slightly emphatic and unemphatic periphrases (2 and 3) are always difficult to distinguish, especially in the absence of evidence about stress and intonation in the earlier periods of the language.

1. *Deliberate emphasis* (as in modern English).

E.M.I.H. V. 3. 224 (282) *Pe.* I beseech your worship to pardon me. *Clem.* Well, sirha tell him I *do* pardon him

Poet. I. 2. 196 (215) Men of worth have their chymæra's, as well as other creatures: and they *doe* see monsters, sometimes: they *doe*, they *doe*

Volp. I. 1. 52 (26) *Mosca.* You lothe, the widdowes, or the orphans teares/Should wash your pavements; or their pittious cryes/Ring in your roofes; and beate the aire, for vengeance.—*Vol.* Right, Mosca, I *doe* lothe it

Epic. II. 6. 26 (197) How the slave *doth* latine it !

2. *With slightly emphatic colour* (now out of date).

C.A. IV. 5. 46 (157) danger *doth* breed delay, love makes me chollericke (rhythm seems to be an added consideration here)

E.M.I.H. I. 1. 172 (202) graunt, that he *doe* turne Foole presently

E.M.O.H. III. 2. 10 (498) I *doe* want yet some fifteene, or sixteene hundred pounds

Poet. II. 1. 73 (223) *Albi.* shee has the most best, true, fæminine wit in Rome ! *Cris.* I have heard so, sir; and *doe* most vehemently desire to participate the knowledge of her faire features

Sej. V. 613 (460) those needfull iealousies of state, that warne wiser princes . . . and *doe* teach them how learned a thing it is to beware of the humblest enemy

Epic. Ded. 7 (161) This makes, that I now number you, not onely in the Names of favour, but the Names of iustice, to what i write; and *doe*, presently, call you to the exercise of that noblest, and manlyest vertue.

Bart. F. I. 6. 64 (38) Truely, I *doe* love my child dearely, and I would not have her miscarry.

Mag. La. Chor. I. 66 (529) Faith we *doe* call a Spade, a Spade, in Cornwall.

3. *Unemphatic* (now out of date).

Modern English has ensured order and clarity by dropping this merely expletive use of *do*. It is not very common in Jonson. Bradley justifies it in the Bible solely on the ground of rhythm.

Bart. F. II. 2. 51 (42) I *doe* water the ground in knots, as I goe.

4. *With inversion of pronominal subject to give special emphasis to some other part of the sentence, the notional verb being placed last.* (Still in use, especially in poetry.)

Volp. I. 4. 110 (39) This plot/*Did* I thinke on before

Bart. F. IV. 6. 169 (112) Mad *doe* they call him !

5. *'Do' for metre* (still used in poetry).

The periphrasis may be also mildly emphatic.

T.T. V. 10. 98 (92) And so *doth* end our Tale, here, of a Tub

E.M.I.H. I. 4. 170 (218) spirits of one kinde and qualitie,/ *Do* meete to parlee

Revels V. 6. 10 (161) Cynthias shining orbe was made/Heaven to cheere, when day *did* close

Poet. I. 1. 53 (208) And so shall Hesiod too, while vines *doe* beare

Alch. I. 1. 27 (296) Where, like the father of hunger, you *did* walk

Cat. II. 1 (454) Those roomes *doe* smell extremely. Bring my glasse

" IV. 855-58 (525) That now *doe* hope, and now *doe* feare,/ And now envy;/ and then *doe* hate, and then love deare,/But know not why:

Stap. N. I. 3. 48 (292) Poore Rascalls, I *doe* doe it out of charity.

(b) Questions

In Jonson, where the question is not introduced by an interrogative word, the periphrastic construction is the more frequent. The reason seems to be that the initial *do* bears the stress, and is therefore emphatic, while also on occasion serving the turn of metre. But an interrogative word used to open a question takes away the stress from the succeeding auxiliary, and its emphatic purpose is lost. The non-periphrastic construction is then favoured.

1. *Periphrastic construction.* (Normal form of modern English, used in 16th C alongside of 2.)

The subject is placed between the auxiliary and the notional verb.

(i) *Where no interrogative word is used*

E.M.I.H. I. 3. 128 (210) *did* you ever see it acted ?

Revels IV. 2. 34 (107) *doe* you interpret for these puppets ?

Poet. Induc. 56 (205) *doe* you hide your selves ?

Epic. I. 2. 62 (172) *Do's* he, that would marry her, know so much ?

Alch. II. 1. 46 (315) *Doe* you thinke, I fable with you ?

Bart. F. III. 5. 39 (74) Ballad-man, *do's* any cutpurses haunt hereabout ?

S.S. I. 5. 81 (20) *Doe* you thinke so ?

(ii) *Introduced by interrogative word*

T.T. V. 4. 11 (82) *how doe* you meane ?

E.M.I.H. I. 3. 32 (207) *why do* you laugh sir ?

Volp. I. 2. 41 (29) into *whom did'st* thou passe ?

Epic. II. 3. 61 (185) *What doe* you think of the Poets, sir Iohn ?

2. *Non-periphrastic construction* (frequent in 16th C, now archaic and poetical).

Here the notional verb is followed by the subject:

(i) *Where no interrogative word is used*

C.A. I. 6. 54 (114) *Lookes* my love well ?
E.M.I.H. V. 1. 63 (272) *saw* you Hesperida ?
Revels IV. 1. 114 (103) *Say* you so ?
Volp. II. 1. 111 (49) *came* you forth/Emptie of rules, for travaile?
Epic. V. 3. 140 (260) shall you ever come to an end, *thinke* you ?
Bart. F. II. 4. 60 (49) *Will* you any tabacco, Master Arthur ?

(ii) *Introduced by interrogative word*

E.M.I.H. I. 3. 111 (209) *How passes* the day abroad sir ?
Poet. I. 1. 43 (207) Envie, *why twitst* thou me ?
Volp. I. 2. 38 (29) *what* body then *tooke* thee ?
Epic. I. 2. 57 (172) *where lyes* shee ?
Alch. V. 1. 27 (388) *when saw* you him ?
S.S. I. 6. 63 (23) And *wherefore think* you so ?

II. NEGATIVE

(*a*) *Statements*

Jonson seems to have preferred the non-periphrastic construction, especially 2 (ii), to the periphrastic, in what might be called his literary manner.

1. *Periphrastic construction.* (Normal form of modern English, taking the place of 2.)

(i) *Usual order*

The modern colloquial contraction of the negative to *n't* does not occur.

E.M.I.H. II. 1. 36 (221) though I *did* not fancie her, yet shee loved mee dearely
Poet. II. 2. 176 (232) all this *doth* not yet make mee envie you
Volp. III. 3. 15 (70) this feat body of mine *doth* not crave
Alch. III. 1. 5 (341) I *doe* not like the man
Cat. V. 225 (534) See, they *doe* not/Die in a ditch

(ii) *With inversion of pronominal subject as in affirmative statements* (see I. a. 4)

This is to give special emphasis to some other part of the sentence.

Epic. IV. 5. 66 (237) but so offended a wight as sir Amorus *did* I *never* see.

8

2. *Non-periphrastic construction* (common in 16th C, especially (ii), but now archaic and poetical).

(i) *Verb preceded by negative* (as in O.E. ʒē ne bǣron)
A very common order in 16th C verse.
T.T. V. 3. 6 (80) I *not* see 'hem,/No creature, but the foure wise Masters here
E.M.I.H. II. 2. 25 (223) Others . . . practise to expell/Their liege Lord Reason, and *not* shame to tread
E.M.O.H. Induc. 51 (430) I *not* observ'd this thronged round till now
Revels I. 5. 34 (62) how . . . base a thing is man,/If he *not* strive
Sej. I. 375 (367) Wee *not* endure these flatteries, let him stand
Alch. II. 2. 55 (344) I *not* denie,/But such as are not graced . . ./ May . . . be adverse in religion.

(ii) *Verb followed by negative.* This was the recognized order of 16th C literary prose, and is often there used in emphatic situations where the periphrastic construction would have been better (see example 4).

E.M.I.H. I. 4. 114 (216) He came *not* to his lodging
Poet. I. 2. 4 (209) the best and gravest Romanes, that you think *not* on
Volp. II. 2. 178 (55) I aske you *not*
Alch. Read. 21 (291) I deny *not*, but that these men . . . may some time happen on some thing that is good.
Bart. F. II. 4. 37 (48)—stage direction—This they whisper, that Overdoo heares it *not*

(b) *Questions*

Here the negative shares the emphasis with the initial word of the question, whether the auxiliary *do* or an interrogative. The periphrastic construction is in both cases preferred.

1. *Periphrastic construction.* (Normal form of Modern English; used in 16th C alongside of 2.)
The usual Elizabethan order was (*a*) *do* (*b*) subject (*c*) negative (*d*) notional verb. Often, however, the negative came immediately after *do*, as in modern English, but the contracted form *don't* did not appear in literature until the latter half of the 17th C (apparently first in the colloquial dialogue of Dryden's plays). Even in modern English *not* after the subject is the order in elegant or literary language.

(i) *Where no interrogative word is used*

(α) *Negative after the subject*

T.T. III. 8. 10 (55) *Do's* hee *not* often come, and visit you ?

E.M.I.H. I. 3. 32 (207) *do* you *not* meane signior Bobadilla ?

Poet. II. 1. 131 (224) *Doe* I *not* beare a reasonable corrigible hand over him, Crispinus ?

Bart. F. IV. 2. 8 (89) *doe* you *not* know him ?

Stap. N. II. 2. 32 (307) *Doe* you *not* know her, Sir, neither ?

Mag. La. IV. 4. 37 (569) *Didst* thou *not* sweare/To keepe it secret ?

(β) *Negative immediately before subject*

T.T. II. 1. 28 (26) *Did not* I tell you o' this ?

C.A. I. 3. 17 (109) *do not* I know you Peter ?

Volp. III. 7. 2 (76) *Did not* I say, I would send ?

Bart. F. II. 2. 63 (43) *did not* I bid you should get this chayre let out o' the sides ?

(γ) Sometimes (as in modern English) the question is put in the form of a positive statement, followed by the auxiliary *do* and the negative.

Sej. V. 880 (469) The multitude ? they reele now ? *doe* they *not* ?

Bart. F. I. 3. 129-130 (26) you thought her name had beene Winnifred, *did* you *not* ?

(δ) Note the attraction (common also in modern English) of the order of the question to that of a statement in the following example. An examination of the context shows that this is not due to the nature of the answer expected.

Revels I. 1. 14 (44) You *did* never steale Mars his sword out of the sheath, you ?

(ii) *Introduced by interrogative word*

In modern English the retention of *not* after the subject, as in Elizabethan English, seems to be designed for rhetorical effect.

T.T. I. 6. 6 (22) *Why* stand you still, and *doe not* call my sonne ?

Alch. II. 3. 171 (326) *who doth not* see, in daily practice,/Art can beget bees

Alch. V. 5. 132 (406) *Why doe* you *not* buckle to your tooles ?

Bart. F. II. 2. 133 (45) *Why dost* thou *not* fetch him drinke ?

„ V. 6. 102 (139) *why dost not* speake

2. *Non-periphrastic construction* (frequent in 16th C, now archaic and poetical).

In both (i) and (ii) the normal Elizabethan order was (1) verb (2) subject (3) negative. But the negative is sometimes found immediately after the verb, as in (i) (β).

(i) *Where no interrogative word is used*
   (α) Alch. IV. 4. 91 (375) *Knew* you *not* that ?
   (β) C.A. III. 3. 44 (143) *remembers not* your Lordship,/That poverty is the precious gift of God,/As well as riches ?

(ii) *Introduced by interrogative word*
   Bart. F. IV. 1. 18 (86) *Why bring* you him *not* up?

B. IMPERATIVE

I. AFFIRMATIVE

The non-periphrastic imperative of modern English is the regular form for affirmative exhortations and commands, e.g. Poet. Induc. 6 (203) Cling to my necke, and wrists, my loving wormes. Examples are numberless and need not be recorded. The pronoun was sometimes inserted after the imperative (see under Pronouns: Personal, § 11) e.g.

E.M.I.H. I. 4. 120 (216) stand *you* away, and you love me (no longer in use).

The following *periphrastic* usages had, in Elizabethan English, as now, specific functions:

1. *'Do' at the beginning*
   The original function of this periphrasis was emphatic, i.e. to strengthen an entreaty, exhortation or command (see examples in *N.E.D.* B. I. 30. a). While it retained this usage in the 16th C, it has usually in Jonson a courteous or pleading significance.

   (i) *With pronoun following* (common in 16th C, but now out of date). The insertion of the pronoun seems to transform the command into a formal instruction or polite request.

   E.M.I.H. I. 4. 6 (213) *do* you see the deliverie of those wares to Signior Bentivole
   Epic. II. 4. 85 (190) *doe* you two entertaine sir Iohn Daw, with discourse

II

Alch. I. 2. 160 (308) *Doe* you but say to me, Captayne, I'll see her Grace.

Bart. F. I. 5. 12 (31) *doe* you shew discretion, though he bee exorbitant

Mag. La. IV. 6. 7 (571) *Doe* you intercept him,/And prevent that.

(ii) *Without pronoun* (common also in modern English). Since the 18th C this usage seems to be confined to instances of entreaty.

Bart. F. I. 5. 88 (33) Why, see it, Sir, see it, *doe* see it !

Stap. N. I. 4. 16 (293) *Doe* good woman, have patience

The distinction between auxiliary and substitute *do* is sometimes not easy to make, as in the following examples:

Poet. I. 2. 32 (210) *Ovid. se.* Sirrah, goe get my horses ready . . . *Tucc. Doe*, you perpetuall stinkard, *doe*, goe, talke to tapsters and ostlers, you slave

Cat. IV. 24 (499) *Doe*; urge thine anger, still

Stap. N. V. 2. 93 (372) *Pic.* I'll . . . sue you all. *P.Ca. Doe, doe*, my gowned Vulture

N. Inn IV. 4. 243 (475) At your owne perill, *doe*, make the contempt.

Mag. La. IV. 2. 54 (566) *Com* . . . Ha' you a Licence ? *Pra.* No;/ But I can fetch one straight. *Com. Doe, doe*, and mind/ The Parsons pint

The pause indicated by the punctuation marks suggests a substitute use, specially emphasized. When *do* is independent of the succeeding notional verb (as here), its usage is generally vicarious. The *N.E.D.* considers that, even in the following (*do but*), *do* was originally a main verb and not an auxiliary:

Sej. I. 267 (364) *Doe but* observe his humour

Volp. III. 7. 111 (80) *Do, but*, go kisse him

Alch. I. 1. 23 (296) *Doe but* collect, sir, where I met you first

Bart. F. IV. 1. 51 (87) *Doe but* shew me Adam Overdoo, and I am satisfied.

D.A. I. 4. 51 (174) *Doe but* talke with him.

2. *'Do' at the end* (common also in modern English). Originally emphatic, now as a sign of encouragement or persuasion. Functionally this use of *do*, like that in 1 (ii) preceding, is probably vicarious.

Revels IV. 3. 368 (120) let him have it . . . if you love me, *doe*, good aunt.

Poet. I. 2. 228 (216) keepe your chamber, and fall to your studies; *doe* so

Epic. I. 2. 54 (172) *Daup.* I'll be innocent. *Tru.* Yes, and be poore, and beg; *doe*, innocent

Bart. F. II. 5. 84 (52) I, I, Gamesters, mocke a plaine plumpe soft wench o' the Suburbs, *doe*

II. NEGATIVE.

The non-periphrastic constructions, especially 2 (ii), were the commoner in the 16th C.

1. *Periphrastic construction* (infrequent in 16th C, now normal usage). This took the place of 2 in ordinary speech. Contraction of negative to *n't* in colloquial literature dates from the late 17th C. *You* after the negative still occurs in Mod. English, e.g. 'Don't *you* tell him' or 'Don't tell him'; but the use of the pronoun seems to have a warning or even threatening significance.

(i) *With pronoun*

Revels IV. 3. 91 (111) But *do not you* change

Volp. II. 7. 101 (65) But *do not you* forget to send, now.

Alch. I. 2. 108 (306) *Do not you* tell him

Bart. F. V. 4. 12 (122) Sir, *doe not you* breed too great an expectation of it

D.A. II. 3. 37 (197) *Doe not you* laugh

Mag. La. II. 5. 60 (538) *Doe not you*/Offer to meddle, let them take their course

(ii) *Without pronoun*

T.T. II. 2. 41 (28) Come Awdrey, *doe not* shake

E.M.I.H. I. 4. 131 (217) *do not* fret your selfe thus

Poet. I. 2. 112 (212) Come, *doe not* mis-prize him

Bart. F. II. 5. 25 (50) *Doe not* see him

2. *Non-periphrastic construction*

(i) *Verb preceded by negative* (infrequent in 16th C and no longer in use).

Revels II. 1. 8 (63) act freely, carelessly, and capriciously . . . and *not* utter a phrase

Volp. II. 5. 68 (61) be not seene, paine of thy life;/*Not* looke toward the windore

(ii) *Verb followed by negative* (usual practice in 16th C, now archaic and poetical).

The object, if there is one, may be placed before or after the negative. The pronominal subject is sometimes inserted.

(a) Transitive verbs

(α) With direct object

C.A. II. 7. 104 (138) *spare not* me
E.M.I.H. I. 1. 6 (197) *disturbe* him *not*
Bart. F. I. 6. 37 (37) *Slander not* the Brethren, wicked one
„ V. 3. 53 (119) *Call* me *not* Leatherhead
S.S. II. 5. 43 (34) *Report not* you your griefes

(β) Without object (or with indirect object only)

E.M.I.H. (F) IV. 2. 71 392 *tell not* me of my money

(b) Intransitive verbs

Poet. Induc. 14 (203) *Wonder not*, if I stare
Epic. IV. 5. 63 (237) *Trust not* you to that visor
Bart. F. V. 6. 93 (139) nay, Sir, *stand not* you fixt here, like
a stake in Finsbury to be shot at

2. NOUNS

2. Appositional accusative

The appositional accusative was known in O.E. after verbs of denotation, e.g. Genesis A 1234 *þone yldestan Noæ* nemde. The construction is described by Maetzner (*English Grammar* II. II. A. p. 195) as a predicative determination. Its scope was somewhat limited in the early history of the language; but in M.E., on the analogy of Latin and other Romance languages, the appositional accusative began to be used after verbs of declaring, considering, showing, etc., and is still in vogue, e.g. I consider *him* a *genius*.

A similar O.E. prepositional construction with *for* and *to* was equally popular in M.E. and E.N.E., e.g.

Beowulf 1175 Þæt þū *for* sunu wolde hererinc habban
Layamon I. 18 Makeden hine *to* duke

In the first of these sentences modern English takes the preposition *as*; in the second, no preposition is required.

In Jonson we find simple apposition where now *as* would be required.

Revels I. 4. 97 (57) talke of some hospitall, whose walls record his *father* a *Benefactor*

3. Ambiguous 'of' with objective genitive

Den Breejen is probably correct in believing the gradual decline of the objective genitive to be due to its possibilities of ambiguity (see *The Genitive and its of-Equivalent*, Ch. VI). The inflected genitive is undoubtedly a more frequent cause of confusion than the substitute-genitive;[1] but the peculiar wording of a sentence may make the latter equally ambiguous, e.g. Romans VIII. 38 I am persuaded that neither death nor life . . . shall be able to separate us from the love *of* God which is in Christ Jesus our Lord. Though Paul probably meant 'the love of God to us', the construction equally suggests 'our love to God'. In such circumstances good modern English would

[1] The original meaning of *of* seems to have been 'away from'; in O.E. it was also frequently used to denote source, origin or birth, and it is from the latter that the wider employment of the substitute genitive (*of* + noun) arose in M.E. under the influence of Fr. *de*.

clarify the construction either by a periphrasis or the use of another preposition. A similar example occurs in Jonson.

E.M.O.H. IV. 4. 117 (543) I love thee above the love *of* women (= my love for women)

4. Descriptive substitute-genitive

The use of the substitute-genitive as a descriptive or qualifying adjective arose in M.E. and increased in E.N.E., partly taking the place of the O.E. inflected genitive of quality, quantity and state (also found in Gothic and other Germanic languages) e.g. *werhādes* and *wīfhādes* hē gescēop hīe; *ānes monðes* fierst. Kellner (*Historical Outlines of English Syntax*, § 166) gives examples of the descriptive substitute-genitive from *Layamon* I. 229 Ælc mon nom ane scale *of rede golde*, and *Malory* 357. 23 She is the fairest lady and most *of beauty* in the world.

Malory's use of the substitute-genitive in place of an adjective, e.g. "a thing of beauty" instead of "a beautiful thing" seems an innovation. The practice was not uncommon in the 16th and early 17th centuries, but has since declined.

E.M.I.H. (F) II. 1. 30 (324) your iudgement is *of strength,*/Against the neerenesse of affection

E.M.O.H. III. 8. 91 (522) is not his authoritee *of power* to give our Scene approbation ? (so Alch. III. 2. 46 (344) and C.A. IV. 4. 26 (155))

Poet. Prol. 17 (205) he doth implore,/You would not argue him *of arrogance*;/How ere . . ./Our frie of writers, may beslime his fame

Bart. F. V. 3. 130 (121) other pretty passages there are . . that will delight you, Sir, and please you *of iudgement*

Sej. III. 48 (394) Nor can I argue these *of weaknesse*; since/They take but naturall wayes

N. Inn III. 2. 2 (451) first produce the parties:/And cleere the court. The time is now *of price.*

S.S. II. 6. 91 (37) me thought it was a sight/*Of joy*, to see my two brave Rammes to fight !

5. Genitive of respect

This function of the genitive is closely related to the last: the inflected form existed in O.E. e.g. *wīges* heard, *wordes* wīs. The substitute-genitive, which took its place in 13th C, is distinguished by the fact that it invariably follows an adjective, having then the function of a qualifying adverb (See *N.E.D.* under *Of*, XI. 35).

Alch. I. 4. 8 (313) Slow *of his feet*, but earnest *of his tongue*
Bart. F. II. 2. 25 (41) though I be a little crooked *o' my body*

Except in particular phrases, e.g. slow *of speech*, this use of the genitive is now obsolescent in prose, its place being taken by parasynthetic adjectival compounds, e.g. *slow-footed*, *earnest-tongued*.

6. Partitive genitive

This is a familiar construction in Latin, Gothic and all the older languages of the West Germanic group, including O.E. An account of it in English is given by Kellner (*H.O.E.S.* §§ 173-176), who shows that this genitive is governed by nouns, pronouns (interrogative and indefinite), numerals, and adjectives in the comparative or superlative degree. In O.E. the partitive genitive was inflexional; but in M.E. (about the 13th C) it became inflexionless, especially after nouns of quantity. By the 14th C it was a common custom to place the partitive element in simple apposition to the governing word, except after *all* and superlative adjectives. A similar decay of this inflexional genitive is found in Old Norse, German and Dutch.

The prepositional partitive seems, from the examples in the *N.E.D.* (see under *Of*, XIII, 42), to have arisen in the transition period (L.O.E.—E.M.E.) by analogy with the Latin use of the preposition *ex* or *de*. It was at first used to denote the land of origin, e.g. Bede: Wǽron þær in þā tiid moniʒe *of Ongelpeode*. By E.N.E. this genitive had begun to show signs of arresting the parallel appositional construction, still used archaically, however, by Spenser (e.g. *F.Q.* I. 3. 37 For he is *one the truest knight* alive) and Jonson (see (*c*) below).

Chaucer and Caxton used a mixed construction, especially after numerals. The influence of the appositional form ("one the greatest author") is clearly indicated in the use of the genitive singular instead of plural, e.g. (the examples are Kellner's)

Chaucer, *N. Priest's Tale*, 164: Oon of the gretteste *auctour* that men rede.

Caxton, *Aymon 272*, 23: But of all france I am one of the best and truest *knyght* that be in it.

Modern English has preserved a few appositions, notably after *dozen* and *score* (e.g. a *dozen loaves*, three *dozen pairs*, three *score years* and ten); but these are no longer regarded as partitive genitives. The inflected plurals, *dozens*, *scores*, however, retain the prepositional partitive (e.g. dozens *of* pairs; scores *of* sheep).

Jonson uses the prepositional partitive after numerals and words of quantity, whether singular or plural. He also uses an elliptical construction, found in the Bible and other 16th C literature, in which the governing word (modern *some* or *one*) appears to be omitted (see (*b*)). Actually these examples illustrate the retention of an old partitive construction, familiar in Chaucer, e.g. Prol. C.T. 146. *Of smale houndes* hadde she.

(*a*) *After words of quantity*
E.M.I.H. II. 3. 116 (229) if I had a million *of lives*
    „   (F) III. 1. 169 (343) a hundred *of lice* goe with him
E.M.O.H. IV. 6. 45 (548) fiftie score *of pounds*
Revels II. 2. 102 (69) in a paire or two of *moneths*
D.A. IV. 4. 94 (238) We may have our doozen *of visiters*
N. Inn III. 1. 192 (450) a dozen *of bawdy songs*

Note: The partitive genitive is not always used, especially after *dozen*:
E.M.I.H. III. 2. 72 (240) a dozen *Gentlemen*
Revels II. 2. 102 (69) halfe a dozen *taffata gownes*

(*b*) *Elliptical partitive*
Revels V. 10. 16 (172) here be *of all sorts*
Epic. II. 3. 110 (186) Why? everyman, that writes in verse, is not a Poet; you have *of the Wits*, that write verses, and yet are no Poets
Cat. I. 484 (450) I' have kill'd a slave,/And *of his blood* caus'd to be mixt with wine
Stap. N. III. 3. 47 (340) Sirs,/You must get *o' this newes*
Mag. La. Chor. I. 26 (528) For there be *of the People*, that will expect miracles
    „   „   II 7. 5 (543) They say you have retain'd brisk Mr Practise/Here, *of your Councell*

Note: The same construction is found with pronouns, e.g.
Volp. II. 6. 8 (62) Corbaccio, and Voltere, brought *of it*;/Whilst I was busie in an inner roome
Cat. IV. 723 (521) There are *of us* can be as exquisite traytors

(*c*) *Appositional construction in poetry*
Sej. V. 59 (438) The fate of *some your servants*
Mag. La. I. 1. 21 (513) I have beene imployed,/By *some the greatest States-men* o' the kingdome

Note: Jonson only uses this appositional construction where the governing word is an indefinite pronoun or adjective.

7. Indirect object following the direct object

In O.E. the dative as indirect object required no preposition. The preposition *to* was at first reserved for the idea of 'motion towards'; but in L.O.E. its use was extended. Verbs of 'giving' in O.E. generally took the dative without preposition.

In M.E. the simple dative became confused with the accusative, and, possibly on the analogy of French *à* (Lat. *ad*), the preposition *to* began to be used with the new 'objective' (Sweet's 'common') case, especially where the indirect object was placed after the direct object; as in Mod. English 'He gave the money *to* the man'. But instances still remained where the dative function could be identified by its original conventional position viz. before the direct object (e.g. He gave *the man* the money), and here the preposition was not generally used, unless special circumstances, such as metrical requirements, called for it; as in Chaucer's *Legend of Good Women* 533: Mars gaf *to hire* corone red parde.

In the examples below from Jonson the indirect object appears last without *to*. This usage is even more common in Shakespeare (see the many citations in Maetzner's *English Grammar* II. II. A, p. 208). The evidence from these two dramatists shows that where the indirect object (whether noun or pronoun) occurs last without *to*, it is because the direct object which precedes it is an unemphatic personal pronoun.

E.M.I.H. I. 3. 198 (212) give it *the gentleman*
,,   (F) I. 2. 119 (310) deliver it *my sonne*

Examples where the indirect object is a pronoun are included for the sake of convenience:
C.A. II. 7. 91 (137) Ile give hem *thee*, I faith
Volp. I. 5. 12 (41) give it *him* (This is still found in Mod. English, but is not very idiomatic)

Note: Where the direct object is a noun clause, its position is usually last:

Cat. II. 128 (458) I yield *you*, it might, at first

8. Relict of old dative of separation

Certain verbs of 'depriving' etc. in O.E. took what may be described as a dative of separation without preposition. The person deprived is in the accusative, and the thing from which separated in the dative e.g. hē hine unscrȳdde ðæm *healfan sciccelse* (he tore from him half of his cloak). This construction

19

was occasionally preserved in M.E. and N.E. An example with relative pronoun *what* (from E.M.O.H.) is here included for the sake of convenience.

E.M.I.H. I. 4. 100 (216) an apt pretext to banish them *my house*
E.M.O.H. III. 8. 44 (520) Restore to all men, *what* with wrong I rob'd
  them (what = that of which; Mod. English would end the
  subordinate clause with *of*)

9. Use of nouns as adjectives

In O.E. poetry compounds of the permanently associated type (e.g. *sceadugenga* = one who walks in darkness, c.f. modern *music-teacher*) were extremely common, and were written as one word. This kind of compounding was a feature of O.E. poetic diction, but comparable uses in prose were rare.

The phenomenon here considered is the free and occasional use of the noun as an adjective, i.e. the case of a noun losing for the nonce its substantiveness and becoming attributive.

In E.N.E. the noun functioned as an adjective very freely— a usage not uncommon in M.E., but much extended in the 16th and 17th centuries. The practice is regarded by Abbott (*Shak. Gram.* § 22) as a licence, a misapprehension probably due to the unfamiliar nature of the nouns employed by Shakespeare. The practice has continued in modern English and has been given a new stimulus by the needs of technical scientific language, e.g. *induction* coil, *magneto* wire, which begin by being loose, and end by becoming permanent, associations.

The freedom with which the Elizabethans used all kinds of nouns as adjectives may have been aided by the earlier habit of employing the uninflected genitive of proper names attributively, which still obtains (e.g. *Cheddar* cheese, *Yorkshire* pigs. Shakespeare has *Tiber* banks, *Tagus* stream, *Tewksbury* mustard, *Cyprus* wars, *Pisa* walls, *Philippi* fields, *Turkey* cushions). Jonson is little behind Shakespeare in his innovations in the form of the noun-adjective.

E.M.I.H. II. 3. 151 (230) a scurvy *rogue* Souldier
  „   III. 1. 166 (237) these leane *rascall* daies
  „   III. 3. 52 (244) an *ingratitude* wretch
  „   III. 4. 130 (251) your *Ruffian* trickes
  „   (F) I. 2. 82 (309) our *Turkie* companie
E.M.O.H. Induc. 165 (434) breakes a drie-*bisquet* iest
Revels IV. 1. 174 (104) one of your *miscelany* madams
Mag. La. III. 5. 25 (554) I' their *swath* bands

10. Use of nouns as verbs

Only less frequent than the above was the use by Shakespeare and Jonson of nouns as verbs. A few instances from Jonson are noted.

Sej. I. 141 (359) both were of best feature, of high race,/*Yeer'd* but to thirtie

S.S. II. 5. 29 (33) Fetch it againe or *kennel* with the hounds

S.S. III. 2. 32 (45) giving to the World/Againe, his first and tunefull *planetting*!

3. PRONOUNS

PERSONAL

11. Emphatic 2nd personal pronoun with imperative

The O.E. negative imperative (*ne* + verb) usually took the pronoun after the verb, e.g. ne helpaþ *gē*.

The O.E. affirmative imperative might or might not employ a pronoun. The use of a pronoun seemed to carry a mild degree of emphasis, e.g. wite *ðū*.

The post-position was not essential in O.E. e.g. *gē* ęfthwęrfað to ciricean. But in N.E. the pre-verb order seems to be used to indicate (*a*) a menacing attitude, e.g. *you* do as you are told, or (*b*) that a distinction of persons is required, e.g. *you* enter first, and I shall follow.

In E.N.E. the pronoun with post-verb position was common in affirmative imperatives. Its use was mainly emphatic. But unemphatic forms, such as *ye* (singular[1]) and the probably dialectal *thee* (for *thou*), were also in regular employment, especially in stock phrases, such as 'hark *ye*' and 'fare *thee* well'. In modern dialect and vulgar speech both of these forms have been levelled to unemphatic *'ee* e.g. hark *'ee*.

The employment of these colloquial, and often ungrammatical, forms in unemphatic positions during the E.N.E. period may have been influenced by the use of the personal for the reflexive pronoun after the imperative of certain verbs, such as *go, hie, haste* and *sit*, e.g. E.M.I.H. I. 2. 11 (203) hie *thee* in again (= thyself).

Idiomatic examples of the emphatic use are still current in modern English, e.g. mind *you*.

    (*a*) *Uses probably emphatic*

        E.M.I.H. I. 1. 204 (202) Take *you* no knowledge I have open'd it
        ,,   I. 4. 120 (216) stand *you* away, and you love me

    (*b*) *Uses probably unemphatic*

        C.A. II. 2. 58 (126) But harke *thee* Rachel: say a theefe should come

---

[1] The nom. plur. *ye* began to be used in the nom. sing. in 13th C. as a term of respect. This use continued in dialect, after it had disappeared in standard English.

12. Case-shifting

The general subject of case-shifting is discussed by Jespersen in *Progress in Language*, Ch. VII. The phenomena and the largely conjectural reasons are so diverse, that it is best to deal with each case as it arises.

Curme (*Grammar of the English Language*, III. 7. c. a) considers that there has been a general tendency in N.E. to use the accusative of personal pronouns as a common case. The commonest instances are predicative, e.g. it wasn't *him*. Curme accounts for this by saying that position after the verb becomes associated with the use of the objective case. But in vulgar speech the usage spread quite early to other positions (see (*a*) (ii)), e.g. *Me* and my mate are of one mind.

Wright's brief summary of the dialectal evidence is interesting (*Dial. Gram.* § 402): "In all the dialects of Sc. and Eng. the objective form of the personal pronoun is used for the nominative:

(1) After the substantive verb, as *it was her that did it*.

(2) When standing alone, as *who did that ?   Her*.

(3) When the verb refers to different persons, as *him and me did it*; *Jack and us went together*."

Jonson, unlike Shakespeare, does not seem to use anything but the nominative after *it* + verb 'to be'. The modern colloquial 'it is *me*', now justified, on the score of usage, by many grammarians (see Jespersen, *Prog. in Language* §§ 184-96) is not found.

Predicative uses of the personal pronoun in the nominative are common:—

T.T. II. 2. 132 (31) That's *he*
E.M.I.H. IV. 2. 99 (261) Its not *he*: is it ?
E.M.O.H. V. 2. 63 (569) This is *he* !
Revels I. 1. 2 (44) Tis *I*, blind archer
Poet. V. 3. 92 (300) That's *I*; I am the wolfe
Sej. IV. 34 (419) We are *they*, he shot at
Bart. F. V. 4. 65 (123) That's *I* (So Stap. N. I. 5. 85 (296))

In other circumstances, however, Jonson does confuse his cases.

(a) *Accusative for nominative*

(i) *After 'here be'*

From examples in the *N.E.D.* it is clear that *them* was used (i) for *they*, and (ii) for *those*, at least as early as the 16th C. Both uses occur in Jonson; and from their prevalence in modern dialect, it is probable that their origin was dialectal. In Elizabethan and Jacobean drama, *them* after 'here (there) be' was an idiomatic colloquialism employed even by the literate. It is difficult to distinguish personal and demonstrative uses; modern English idiom has *those who* for *they*. *Those* + relative pronoun was certainly in use before the 16th C.

> E.M.I.H. I. 1. 90 (199) here be *them* can perceive it (Used by Stephano)
> „ V. 3. 49 (277) here be *them* have beene amongst souldiers (Used by Dr. Clement)
> Gypsies Metamorphosed 918 (596) S'lid, here be *them* can loose a purse in honor of the Gypsies (Used by Puppy, a clown)

Note: The colloquialism is by no means consistently used, e.g.

> Revels IV. 3. 337 (119) heere be *they* will swallow anything

(ii) *Dialectal and vulgar accusative when verb 'to be' refers to different persons*

This peculiarity, as Wright points out (*vide supra*), is common to all dialects of England when the compound subject of the verb 'to be' refers to different persons. The predication is also in the Accusative. The usage still obtains in vulgar colloquial speech.

> N. Inn II. 3. 11 (428) *Tru.* What trick is this . . ./You'ld put upon us ? *Pru.* Us ? Do you speake plurall ? *Tru.* Me and my mares are *us*. *Pru.* If you so ioyne 'hem (The speaker is Trundle, the coachman)

(iii) *Shall us*

Us for *we* occurs six times in Shakespeare after *shall*; also in the vulgar speech of Dickens's novels. It is infrequent in Jonson. Samuel Pegge in his *Anecdotes of the English Language* (1803) draws attention to the fact that the Londoner of his time also used it after the common auxiliaries *can, have, may*. It is notable that *us* only occurs in the post-position; it is, therefore, unemphatic, and is often in 16th and early 17th century drama weakened to *'s*, e.g. *shall's*.

Wright (*Dial. Gram.* § 402) notes that the "objective forms are often used for the nominative when the pronouns are unemphatic, especially in the south-midland, eastern, southern and south-western counties".

Jespersen, on the other hand, considers that, as four of the examples of *shall us* in Shakespeare are equivalent to *let us*, the idiomatic use of the accusative in the former is due to a blending of the two expressions (see *Prog. in Lang.* § 186).

Abbott argues more plausibly (*Shak. Gram.* § 215) that the original meaning of *shall* was one of obligation, and that as there was no action on the part of the subject, the verb became impersonal like the Latin *oportet*, e.g. Chaucer, *us oughte*. He notes, however, that this use is peculiar to the South of England.

Stap. N. IV. 1. 3 (345) what shal's doe with our selves.

(b) *Nominative for accusative: second of two objects in nominative when governed by a verb or preposition*

Both Jonson and Shakespeare have the ungrammatical, but in the 16th and 17th centuries frequently used, nominative case in this position. The fault was a common one among Elizabethan and Jacobean writers, and three explanations are possible:—(α) The intervention of the conjunction (or other words) may have obscured the grammatical relationship of the second object to the governing verb or preposition. This was especially liable to happen when the first object had no inflexional modification to distinguish it as an accusative case. (β) As Jespersen has pointed out (*Prog. in Language*, § 192), the use of *I* as object in the second position may simply have been due to the influence of conventional word order. It was polite to place the first person last, and nominative uses would occur so frequently as to make the *I* combination habitual, in spite of grammatical function. (γ) Its employment may have been an idiomatic licence, somewhat similar to Shakespeare's conscious use of the nominative for rhyme in Sonnet 72:

Unless you would devise some virtuous lie
And hang some praise upon deceased *I*.

An attempt has been made to justify *I* as emphatic in the expression 'between you and I'. The nominative of the first personal pronoun is certainly more emphatic than is the nominative of the third personal pronoun; and it is notable that Jonson only employs this case-shifting with the 1st personal pronoun.

But Jonson, scholar though he was, is by no means exempt from grammatical solecisms. Dryden, discussing the refinement of the language in the 17th C (see *Dramatic Poetry of the Last Age*), gives several instances of obscure and faulty syntax from a few pages of *Catiline*, some of which are noted in this study.

(i) *After verbs*
Revels I. 4. 50 (55) pray you make this gentleman and *I* friends
Note: The following nonce-use after *have* seems to be a grammatical oversight occasioned by the breaking off of a speech.

> N. Inn II. 1. 24 (424) *Lad*. I'le ha' the Lease of his house cut out in measures./*Pru*. And *he* be strangled with 'hem (Here *he* is a grammatical error for *him*, as it is really the object of *have*, to be supplied from the preceding sentence.)

(ii) *After prepositions*
E.M.I.H. V. 3. 141-2 (280) Musco has beene with my cosen and *I* all this day
Sej. V. 670 (462) Why, Macro,/It hath beene otherwise, betweene you and *I* (Abbott, *S.G.* § 205, considers that this had idiomatic sanction in Elizabethan times)
Cf. *The London Prodigal* IV. 3. 78 can disguise your face/From *I* that know you

13. Personal pronouns qualified by adjectives

Franz (*S.G.* § 290) regards this as a substantival use of the personal pronoun, and says that it appears mainly with the 1st person. When the adjective qualifies *he* or *she*, he maintains, the sex is specially emphasized. This is particularly the case in the example from *Bartholomew Fair*, where *she* is clearly substantival, meaning 'woman'. In every case the pronoun is emphatic.

The use of *he* or *she* as a noun was still common in the 19th C (see *N.E.D.* under *She*, IV).

T.T. III. 4. 17 (48) Now stand I vore her, what zaith velvet *she* ?
Poet. III. 4. 49 (247) Was ever wretch so wretched, as unfortunate *I* ?
Volp. I. 3. 47 (34) Happy, happy, *me* ! (This use of *me* in interjectional phrases is apparently influenced by the Latin, e.g. *me* miserum !)
Bart. F. IV. 3. 3 (92) I am no *she*, that affects to be quarell'd for (cf. *Taming of the Shrew* III. 2. 236 the proudest *he*/That stops my way in Padua. Ben Jonson on Shakespeare: that *he*/Who casts to write a living line must sweat).
   Note: Similar restrictive uses, emphasizing the sex, occur with preceding definite article or demonstrative:
N. Inn III. 2. 99 (454) The *he*, or *she*, that loves, engraves or stamps/ Th'Idea of what they love, first in themselves
Golden Age Restored 57 (423) which of you is that *hee*,/Would not himselfe the weapon bee,

14. Use of personal pronoun qualified by following prepositional phrase

This construction was already in use in L.M.E., e.g. Mandeville, *Travels*, ch. xxx, 5, þei of Caspye schull gon out (see other examples in H. J. v. d. Meer's *Syntax of Mandeville's Travels*, § 217); and it is fairly common in both Shakespeare and Jonson. The qualifying prepositional phrase is placed after the personal pronoun and is descriptive. The prepositional genitive of origin, birth, race or place is most in use. It is a literary device, not in modern use, except in poetry.

C.A. II. 7. 14 (135) *Sebast* . . . have they their masters of defence in other countries as we have here in Italy ? *Valen.* O Lord, I, especially *they* in Utopia.

15. Use of personal pronoun (or its possessive or reflexive) in following up indefinite pronoun 'one'

The use of the O.E. numeral *ān* as an indefinite pronoun dates from E.M.E.; in O.E. the word *man* was used. Examples cited in the *N.E.D.* show that from the 13th to the 18th C the indefinite *one* was usually referred to by a 3rd personal pronoun such as *his* or *himself*. The same usage is found in the colloquial and literary English of American fiction. The first consistent use of *one* in a sentence quoted by the *N.E.D.* is found in Ritchie's *Wanderings by Seine* (1834): *One's* brothers and sisters are a

part of *one's* self. So that the rigid insistence by Fowler and
other grammarians on *one* throughout, would appear to be un-
historical. Though justified by a modern sense of correctness,
it is avoided by many writers when the repetition of *one* would
be foolishly punctilious and monotonous. The numeral *one* is
correctly followed in modern English by *his*, e.g. *one* brought
his fiddle, another his flute.

The use of the plural pronoun *they, them, their* after *one* was
quite frequent from the 17th C, e.g. 1648 Kenelm Digby's *Private
Memoirs* (255): Hereby *one* may take to *themselves* a lesson.
Colloquially this is still current, and the *N.E.D.* ascribes it to
the indefiniteness of gender of the plural pronoun. The same
construction occurs with *everyone*, e.g. *Everyone* can get the news
for *themselves*; though this usage is now regarded as ungrammatical.

The reflexive pronoun *oneself* is first cited in the *N.E.D.* in 1621.
It does not appear in Shakespeare or Jonson.

(i) *Singular*
    E.M.I.H. I. 4. 181 (218) Shall checke occasion, as *one* doth *his*
        slave
    Poet. IV. 1. 30 (263) how must *one* behave *her selfe* amongst 'hem ?

(ii) *Plural*
    T.T. II. 4. 63 (132) You can constraine *one* ere *they* be aware,/To
        run mad for your love
    S.S. I. 6. 37-8 (22) You stop *ones* mouth,/And yet you bid *'hem*
        speake

16. Erroneous use of personal pronoun for possessive in partitive genitive function

Den Breejen in his work on *The Genitive and its Of- Equivalent in
the latter half of the 16th Century* has a chapter (XI) on the partitive
and possessive functions combined. Examples like "an ungodly
and wycked desyre *of you*" are not uncommon even after the
period with which he deals, and are grammatically justifiable.
He has no example like the following, which is ambiguous and
grammatically unjustifiable.

Cat. II. 167 (460) I can have secret fellowes,/With backs worth ten
    of him (the comparison is not with the persons but with the *backs*
    of the persons. *His* is therefore required).

17. Use of personal pronoun where modern English has the demonstrative

The use of the personal pronoun in conjunction with numerals is infrequent in Jonson. In modern English it occurs chiefly in vulgar speech.

Stap. N. Intermeane I. 9 (302) *they* two help him to a wife

18. Pleonastic pronominal subject or object

(*a*) *The subject pronoun is repeated at the end for emphasis*

In Elizabethan drama a personal pronoun is often found repeated at the end of the sentence for the sake of emphasis (cf. modern dialectal and vulgar "I likes her I do" and "I cares for nobody, no not *I*"). Wright (*Dial. Gram.* § 402) finds that the Northern dialects often use a redundant pronoun at the end in "recriminatory talk". In Jonson the repetition is usually an indication that the emotion of the speaker has been aroused. This emphatic repetition is not to be confused with the resumptive use of the personal pronoun (see (*b*)) common in O.E. and M.E., e.g. Robert of Gloucester 120: þe kyng *hē* sende after him.

C.A. I. 2. 76 (108) . . . *I* care not for the Gentleman *I*, . . .
E.M.I.H. I. 1. 40 (198) . . . *I* scorne it *I*, so *I* doe, . . .
   „   I. 3. 35-36 (207) I dare be sworne, *hee* scornes thy house *hee*.
E.M.O.H. I. 2. 128 (448) . . . *they* are ten times more placable, *they*; . . .
   „   V. 2. 129 (571) Out, *you* foole, *you*.
Bart. F. I. 4. 19 (28) *I* know nothing, *I*, what tell you mee of knowing?

Note: (i) Occasionally the subject is a noun instead of a pronoun, e.g.
C.A. II. 2. 27 (127) . . . the *fellow* talkes in quiddits, *he*

(ii) Ellipsis of the first pronoun and its verb occurs once:
Revels III. 1. 19 (82) *Amo.* Where eate you today? *Aso.* Where you please, sir, any where, *I* ('I eat' is understood after 'sir')

(iii) Repetition of a demonstrative pronoun is also found:
E.M.I.H. I. 4. 132 (217) *These* are my brothers consorts *these*, these are his Cumrades, . . .

(*b*) *Substantival or pronominal subject followed by personal pronoun*

This is probably of dialect origin, and was originally emphatic. Wright (*Dial. Gram.*, § 402) says that "In all the dialects of Sc. and Eng. there is a tendency to introduce a redundant personal pronoun after a noun when emphasis is required; this is especially frequent after a proper name, as *Mr. Smith, he came to my house"*. The original subject may also be a pronoun.

This construction, which is found in O.E., greatly increased its range in the 16th and 17th centuries. It could be used in emotionally vivid passages (i.e. for emotional emphasis) or merely for the sake of metre. As a metrical licence, it was still in vogue among the poets of the 19th C. Colloquially it remains in use in uneducated speech.

(i) *To indicate an agitated or vivid state of mind of a speaker*
 E.M.I.H. IV. 1. 28 (257) I was going along in the streete, thinking nothing, when (of a suddayne) one calls, Signior Lorenzos man: another, *he* cries, souldier
 „   IV. 2. 118 (262) your consort *hee* is gone ? had he stayd he had shard with you infaith

(ii) *Emphatic*
 E.M.I.H. V. 3. 173 (280) now my maister *he* to maintayne the iest, went thether
 Alch. III. 2. 27 (343) As, put the case,/That some great man in state, *he* have the gout

(c) *Substantival subject or object followed by personal pronoun in anacoluthic sentences*
Some unusual constructions employing a redundant personal pronoun are clearly anacoluthic. In the example from *Sejanus* the aim is to avoid the passive construction, in order that the active 'sway him' may rhyme with 'obey him'.

Sej. III. 659 (416) The prince, that feeds great natures, *they* will sway him;/Who nourisheth a lyon, must obey him (The sentence, of which *prince* is the subject, is grammatically incomplete. *They* stands for 'great natures'. In modern English we should write 'The prince that feeds great natures will be swayed by them.')
Epic. I. 1. 54 (166) O, Clerimont, this time, because *it* is an incorporeall thing, and not subject to sense, we mocke our selves the fineliest out of *it*, with vanitie
Cat. III. 221 (476) The fire you speake of,/If any flame of it approach my fortunes,/Ile quench *it*, not with water, but with ruine.

(*d*) *Redundant object anticipating noun clause*

Verbs of thinking, knowing, hearing, perceiving, ascertaining, governing a noun clause, were in 16th and 17th centuries often immediately followed by a personal pronoun as a pleonastic object, e.g. I know *him* what he is.   The construction, which Abbott (*S.G.* § 414) regards as an irregularity, was very useful in verse.

C.A. I. 9. 8 (119) O Francisco, you knew *her* what she was !
Volp. I. 4. 54 (37) You hardly can perceive *him*, that he breathes
Epic. V. 3. 135 (260) have you ever examin'd *her* what religion shee is of ?

(*e*) *Redundant use of personal pronoun as subject or object after long intervening expression*

One would naturally think that the redundant pronoun is brought in to make the meaning clearer.   But this is by no means certain.   In Elizabethan prose one finds surprising ability to carry the meaning in the mind for a long and wheeling flight.   It is possible, then, that this repetition in the form of a pronoun was a conversational trick, sometimes emphatic, as in the example from *Cynthia's Revels* under (ii). H. J. v. d. Meer calls this a 'resumptive' use, and finds that it is already in employment in *Mandeville's Travels* (see his *Syntax of Mandeville's Travels*, § 223).

(i) *Redundant subject*

C.A. IV. 6. 16 (158) You shall have some that had *they* but one quarter/Of your faire beauty, *they* would make it shew/A little otherwise

(ii) *Redundant object*

E.M.I.H. V. 5. 62-3 (401) keepe Cob, and his wife companie, here; *whom*, I will intreat first to bee reconcil'd: and you to endeavour with your wit to keepe '*hem* so
Revels V. 6. 99 (164) *What other things*/Of farther note, doe lye unborne in him,/*Them* I doe leave for cherishment to shew

(*f*) *Redundant uses of 'it'*

These uses are mainly idiomatic and are designed (i) to place the real subject or object in an unusual, and therefore emphatic, position; and (ii) to signalize a following noun clause or phrase.

(i) *As preparatory subject*

This, of course, is quite common in modern English with noun clauses, e.g. *it* is a pity, that he should fail.

E.M.O.H. I. 3. 65 (454) Is'*t* not pleasing this ? (Here the placing of the demonstrative 'this' last gives it emphasis)

(ii) *As preparatory object*

Here *it* is usually anticipatory of a noun clause or phrase.

Cf. *Beowulf* 1392 Ic *hit* þē gehāte: nō hē on holm losaþ.

E.M.I.H. I. 1. 40 (198) I scorne *it* I, so I doe, to be a consort for every hum-drum

,,   I. 4. 68 (215) tell him of *it*, how he disquiets your house

E.M.O.H. II. 3. 200 (476) here be some slight favours of hers, sir, that doe speake *it*, shee is

Alch. IV. 1. 13 (359) You know *it*/How scrupulous he is

(iii) *After a noun, pronoun, noun clause or phrase*

This is similar to the last, but placing the noun clause or phrase first gives it special emphasis.

C.A. I. 6. 27 (113) How well you are receiv'd in my affection,/ Let *it* appear by this one instance

E.M.I.H. III. 6. 9 (255) What you have possest me withall, Ile discharge *it* amply

,,   IV. 2. 25-6 (259) to come to a publique schoole, they should pardon me, *it* was opposite to my humour

Volp. II. 6. 63 (64) He knowes the state of 's bodie, what *it* is.

,,   IV. 3. 24 (97) I'le trie your salt-head,/What proofe *it* is against a counter-plot.

Epic. V. 4. 217 (270) I'll not trouble you, till you trouble me with your funerall, *which* I care not how soon *it* come. (The relative *which* is the normal subject of *come*; *it* is pleonastic.)

Mag. La. IV. 7. 59 (574) What's done, and dead, let *it* be buried.

19. Idiomatic (and now obsolete) uses of personal pronoun as antecedent of relatives 'that', 'which', 'who'

(*a*) *He* (*him*) *that*

Uses of the personal pronoun followed by a defining relative clause, as illustrated below, are now usually obsolete or literary, e.g. *He that* fights and runs away, lives to fight another day. For *he* we now employ such indefinite expressions as *a man* or *the one*, if a noun has gone before to which *one* can refer, e.g. This gentleman, and *the one that* (*who*) came yesterday, are brothers. The use of *a man that* alongside of *he that* occurs at least as early as L.M.E. (See H. J. v. d. Meer's *Syntax of Mandeville's Travels* §§ 220 and 221).

In predicative uses, where the personal pronoun is emphatic, *he that* (*who*) is still current, e.g. I like James. It is not *he that* (*who*) could have spread the story.

In Jonson *he* is generally followed by *that*, not *who*.

E.M.I.H. (I¹) I. 2. 132 (310) He, *that's* compell'd to goodnesse, may be good.

„ (F) II. 5. 44-5 (335) I thanke heaven, I never yet was *he*,/ *That* travail'd with my sonne.

„ (F) III. 3. 15 (346) Who will not iudge *him* worthie to be rob'd,/*That* sets his doores wide open to a thiefe

Revels II. 1. 69 (65) Here *hee* comes, *that* is all this

Volp. IV. 5. 100 (102) can any man imagine/That *he* will spare 'his accuser, *that* would not/Have spar'd his parent ?

Epic. V. 3. 96 (259) If *shee* prove stubborne, or head-strong, *that* you thought obedient

(b) It . . . that (which)

The use of *it* as antecedent to *that* (*which*) was originally emphatic. It did not survive the 17th C, partly because the neuter personal pronoun tended more and more to fall into unemphatic employment.

In all circumstances *it that* is now superseded by the interrogative-relative *what*.

E.M.I.H. (F) II. 1. 71-2 (325) *It* will never out o' the flesh *that's* bred i' the bone

E.M.O.H. V. 7. 48-9 (587) '*tis* all readie below, *that* was bespoken

Poet. Induc. 3-4 (203) this is *it*,/*That* our sunke eyes have wak't for

Note: Sometimes the relative is omitted:—

Epic. V. 3. 206 (262) O, this was *it*, I fear'd

Bart. F. V. 2. 26 (114) this was *it* you mark'd

(c) They or them . . . that (who)

Except in predicative uses which are also emphatic (vide *he that*), the demonstrative *those* has in modern English superseded the personal pronoun.

Discoveries 176-7 (568) But they *that* seeke Immortality, are not onely worthy of leave, but of praise.

Revels III. 4. 107 (93) Let *them* be good *that* love me, though but few

Epic. II. 3. 111 (186) *they* are poets *that* live by it

Pleasure Reconciled to Vertue 230 (487) *they who* are bred/within the hill/of skill,/ may safely tread/what path they will

Note: Here, too, the relative is sometimes omitted.

Cat. II. 138 (459) There are *they*/Can speake greeke too, if need were

„ III. 643 (490) they are *they*/Must make our peace with him

20. Idiomatic uses of 'it' no longer found

(a) *As subject of predicative verbs followed (sometimes preceded) by descriptions of persons*

Shakespeare and Jonson use this mainly when the person is spoken of contemptuously, or as a child. The source of it may be French *c'est*. It survives in modern English only where the predication is generalized, not particular, e.g. *it* is a wise father that knows his own son.

E.M.I.H. II. 3. 183 (231) *it*s a pretious foole
E.M.O.H. I. 2. 231 (451) *t*is an open-throated, black-mouth'd curre
(refers to Carlo Buffone)
Alch. II. 6. 79 (340) *It* is the gooddest soule
Bart. F. I. 3. 135 (27) A notable hypocriticall vermine *it* is; I
know him
N. Inn I. 3. 5 (410) O Lord, Sir, he prates Latine/And '*t*were a
parrot, or a play-boy.

(b) *Conceptional use of 'it' as object after certain verbs*

The special use of the neuter 3rd personal pronoun illustrated below is termed "unspecified or conceptional *it*" by Jespersen (*Philos. of Grammar*, p. 242). It was more commonly employed in the 16th and 17th centuries than it is today, and some uses go back at least as far as M.E. (with a few doubtful examples in O.E.). There are parallel constructions in early French and German.

A sound historical explanation of this conceptional use of *it* is wanting and the subject needs detailed investigation. Two broad, but not easily stated, divisions suggest themselves. In examples such as 'I'll have *it* out with him' the reference is to a more or less definite conception (= our points of disagreement) or situation. In expressions like 'You'll get *it*', 'we had to foot *it*' or 'go *it* !' the object *it* is what Curme (*G.E.L.*, vol. III § 11. 2 (*b*)) describes as "a convenient complement of transitive and intransitive verbs without definite reference". It would seem that in the second group an important semantic change has taken place. What it is, and how it came about, are really the crux of the matter.

(i) *'It' for an unnamed, but understood, conception or situation*
The usage occurs with both transitive verbs and nor-

mally intransitive verbs used transitively. By modern standards this use of *it* is often pleonastic.

E.M.I.H. V. I. 76 (272) Nay you shall answere *it*, I chardge you goe (i.e. before the court)

,, (F) IV. 5. 10 (371) Ile discharge it amply, sir. Make *it* no question (pleonastic)

E.M.O.H. II. 3. 173 (475) Lord (and 't be thy will) prosper *it* (use with intransitive verb, cf. the modern exhortation 'go it !')

(ii) *'It' as object without definite reference*

In sentences such as "He lords *it* over us", *it* is simply a syntactical device. Two explanations may be offered. In Kellner's view (*H.O.E.S.* § 283), *it* is a substitute for the cognate accusative. The cognate accusative, he says, provides "the idea of any activity as its own object", e.g. he fights *the fight*. But as languages develop, such expressions come to be regarded as tautological, and at this stage the substitute pronoun (English *it*) is called into service for the cognate object, e.g. he fights *it*.

This explanation seems very improbable. A better one is offered by the *N.E.D.* (*It* B. II. 9), though the significance of *it* is not explained. *It* was first used after transitive verbs and followed by the adverb *out*, e.g. to *fight it out*. Later, by the middle of the 16th C, *out* was omitted and the use of *it* mistakenly extended to intransitive verbs, e.g. to *flaunt it*, and to nouns used as verbs, e.g. to *lord it*. A rider is added: *do it* was often used, not only as a substitute for a transitive verb + object, but also for an intransitive verb of action, e.g. he tried to *swim*, but could not *do it*. *It* refers to the activity of 'swimming', and the construction may have influenced the use of *it* in other situations.

If the latter part of the *N.E.D.*'s explanation is accepted, *it* may originally have stood for a definite thing or situation.

The frequency with which this construction occurs with nonce-formations of verbs from nouns, used transitively, gives rise to another suggestion. Jespersen (*Essentials of English Grammar* § 16. 18) considers that this neutral *it* was supplied as object to give the borrowed verb its force, there being no suffix to distinguish it from the noun. As the first example shows, however, this is not necessarily the case—a distinguishing suffix is sometimes also supplied.

Nonce verbs, especially from nouns, were extremely common in the Elizabethan and Jacobean drama, and the use of *it* is most frequently after verbs of this type. It was clearly a colloquial habit, and the *N.E.D.* notes that its survival in modern English is purely a colloquial usage.

Several authorities, notably Franz (*S.G.* § 295), point out that when the construction with *it* occurs after nonce-verbs from nouns that denote classes of persons, e.g. to *lord it*, the action denotes 'behaving in the characteristic manner of'.

T.T. II. 7. 53 (136) Ile beare thy charges and thou wilt but *pilgrimize it* along with me
E.M.I.H. (F) V. 5. 52 (401) penitently *fast it* out in my court
E.M.O.H. V. 2. 60 (568) shall we see him *clowne it*
Volp. III. 7. 5 (77) A courtier would not *ply it* so, for a place
Epic. V. 1. 28 (251) let's *wanton it* and talke waggishly
Alch. IV. 7. 54 (384) that, which the uncleane birds . . ./Were seene to *pranke it* with, on divers coasts
Bart. F. I. 2. 26 (21) that her mother might *hood it*, and *chaine it*, with Mistris Over-doo
Note: Less frequently the same use of *it* occurs after verbs formed from adjectives, e.g. modern English 'to *rough it*'.
Cat. II. 225 (462) What! doe you *coy it*

(iii) *Appositional 'it'*

This occurs mainly after an infinitive phrase. In modern English the preposition *to* is employed in order to avoid repeating the phrase (e.g. I have never built a boat, but I shall try *to*). In Elizabethan English, and sometimes in modern English, *it* replaces *to*.

Sej. IV. 415 (432) One day hee's well; and will returne to Rome:/The next day, sicke; and knowes not when to hope *it*.

(c) *In objective case after prepositions*

Certain idiomatic uses are found in modern English, e.g. Make a day of *it*.
E.M.I.H. I. 4. 158 (218) How e're I set a face on '*t* to the world

21. Uses of dative now obsolete

(a) *Indirect object after certain verbs*

An indirect object can still be used after the verb *tell*, but not after the verbs *say* and *speak*. Examples of the usage were fairly common in the Elizabethan and Jacobean drama.

C.A. II. 1. 14 (125) I marvell, why these gallant youths/Spoke *me* so faire

„ IV. 9. 17 (164) Sayest thou *me* so, mad Greeke ?

E.M.I.H. I. 1. 118 (200) I crye *you* mercy, sir (Abbott, *S.G.* § 201 says that *mercy* is the direct object, as is shown by the shorter form 'cry mercy')

Poet. II. 1. 147 (225) When they come, speake *them* as faire, and give them the kindest welcome in wordes

Mag. La. V. 5. 28 (584) I did long to tell it *you*

(b) *Dative of advantage*

The person to whose advantage or disadvantage a thing is done is placed in the dative. This function of the case was found in O.E. and is still in use, though generally now with the preposition *for*.

N. Inn II. 1. 33 (424) 'Tis rich enough! But 'tis not what I meant *thee!*

(c) *Ethic dative*

The use of this subjective dative reaches its height in the drama of the Elizabethan and Jacobean periods. It is a colloquial usage and is very common in dialect. In the drama it occurs chiefly in vivid passages, indicating rising emotion on the part of the speaker. Hence its prevalence with the pronouns of the first and second person, the speaker or the listener being supposed to have a sympathetic interest in the relation.

The ethic dative is found in Latin and M.E.; Kellner (*H.O.E.S.* § 192) cites an example with the third person from *The Story of Genesis and Exodus* 2495: Hure sinne ðu *him* forgive (forgive us our sins *for his sake*). But examples in O.E. are rare and often open to doubt. The genuine ethic dative seems to have come into literary use in M.E., e.g. *Gawayne and the Green Knight* 1905: And woried *me* þis wyly wyth a wroth noyse.

The ethic dative is, in some instances, very like the dative of advantage, though disadvantage may be implied. In other examples it appears to be pleonastic.

T.T. I. 1. 79 (13) Hee 'll weepe *you*, like all aprill
E.M.I.H. I. 3. 26 (207) upsolve *me* that now (= for me)
   ,,   II. 3. 124 (229) they had planted *me* a demy culvering, iust in the mouth (disadvantage)
E.M.O.H. III. 1. 29 (497) he will sit *you* a whole afternoone sometimes, in a booke-sellers shop, reading the Greeke, Italian, and Spanish (pleonastic)
Volp. III. 4. 118 (74) and he/Would lie *you* often, three, foure houres together,/To heare me speake
Epic. I. 1. 64 (166) Talke *me* of pinnes, and feathers, and ladies, and rushes, and such things: and leave this Stoicitie alone
Bart. F. I. 4. 80 (29) hee will whistle *him*, and all his tunes over, at night in his sleepe !

22. Idiomatic omission of personal pronoun

(a) Subject

Subject omissions occur in Shakespeare and Jonson under various conditions:

(i) In near-formulas and in incomplete colloquial speech, cf. modern 'thank you';

(ii) before *would* in the sense of 'wish';

(iii) frequently in questions in the 2nd person singular.

Jonson's uses fall mainly under the first head.

Wright (*Dial. Gram.* § 402) notes that, at the beginning of a sentence, the pronoun is often omitted in the Southern and S.W. dialects.

(i) E.M.I.H. I. 3. 99 (209) *please* you sit downe (= may it please)
   ,,   (F) I. 2. 46 (308) *crie* you mercie sir (Q. *I* crie you mercy)
   ,,   (F) I. 3. 4 (311) What countenance (*pry'* thee) made he
   ,,   (F) V. 4. 12 (399) *Gi'* you joy
Poet. II. 2. 124 (230) *Ovid.* A song ? come, he shall not denie her. Hermogenes ? *Herm.* '*Cannot* sing. (clipped colloquial speech or possibly petulance)
Alch. II 6. 72 (339) '*Shalt* give his worship, a new damaske suite

(ii) E.M.I.H. I. 4. 159 (218) *Would* I had lost this finger

(iii) C.A. IV. 3. 10 (152) Sirrah Onion, whither *goest* ?

(b) Object

The omission is confined to *it*; the cause was probably lack of emphasis. In N.E. the idiomatic use of *it* in unemphatic positions was greatly increased; and it was therefore an easy step to omit the neuter pronoun altogether.

E.M.I.H. I. 4. 135 (217) let me not live, and I could not finde∧ in my hart to swinge the whole nest of them
E.M.O.H. III. 9. 34 (524) Give ∧ me
,, V. 6. 47 (583) get me somewhat a lesse dog, and clap∧ into the skin

EMPHATIC AND REFLEXIVE

23. The history of the emphatic and reflexive pronoun

In the sentence 'I *myself* saw him', *myself* is heavily stressed, and is emphatic; whereas in 'I hurt *myself*' the stress normally falls on the verb, and *myself* is reflexive. For the sake of convenience, and because their history is related, the two forms are treated together.

In O.E. *self* was used mainly as a strong adjective; there was also a weak form *selfa*, identical in function. This function seems to have been twofold: (*a*) it was commonly placed after a pronoun or noun to emphasize it, (*b*) it was often placed before a noun with the meaning of 'same', 'very'. For the latter there exists in modern English a compound equivalent, e.g. on the *selfsame* day. We are concerned here only with the former or emphatic use, and its subsequent development as a reflexive pronoun. Examples are taken largely from the *N.E.D.* or from Kellner (*H.O.E.S.* §§ 290-300).

(a) Emphatic uses of self

The emphatic use of *self* corresponded almost exactly with that of Lat. *ipse*. O.E. forms were inflected and agreed with the nouns or pronouns they were intended to strengthen.

With noun. Found from O.E. to the 16th C, e.g.

Cynewulf (c 900) *Christ* 134. Nū is rodera Weard, God *sylfa* mid us.
Spenser (1579) *Shep. Cal.*, June 18. This is . . . spoken of the Poete *selfe*.

With personal pronoun (i) In nominative. Common in O.E.,

D

less frequent in Layamon and *Cursor Mundi*, and not found at all in the *Ormulum* (see Kellner § 293). Examples in N.E. are rare.

Beowulf 595. Swa þū *self* talast.

P. Fletcher, *Pisc. Eclog.* IV. 20 *Self* did I see a swain not long ago.

(ii) In oblique cases generally. This occurs in King Alfred, and is found as late as 1576. It was apparently during the 12th C that *self* first began to appear uninflected in oblique cases.

K. Alfred, *Gregory's Past. Care* XXXIII, 220 Đurh þā wē forlǣtaþ ðone anwald *ūre selfra*.

Fleming (1576) *Panopl. Epist.* 24, Wilt thou, Servius, stay *thee self*.

(iii) In pleonastic (or ethic) dative, mainly with intransitive verbs. *Self* is at first an absolute pronoun in apposition to the subject, but placed immediately after the ethic dative, e.g. Earle, *Land Charters* (c. 853) 343 Ealle ðā gerihte ðā ic *mēseolf* ǣr āhte. (This early example is significant for three reasons (*a*) its modern word order (*b*) *mēseolf* written as one word (*c*) its occurrence with a transitive verb. *Mēseolf* can only be explained as an ethic dative of the personal pronoun + *seolf*. It is unlikely that *seolf* is an uninflected dative).

K. Alfred, *Orosius* 66. 6 And him *self* siþþan tō þǣm rīce fēng (subject pron. omitted; *self* is nom. sing.)

K. Alfred, *Boethius* XXI, Hī . . . weorþaþ *him selfe* tō nauhte (*Selfe* is nom. plur. qualifying *hī*)

Probably owing to its idiomatic position, *self* was soon regarded as qualifying the ethic dative. Historically this dative is the forerunner of the compound pseudoreflexive emphatic pronoun of N.E., e.g. he did it *himself*; similarly, by analogy, of *herself*, *itself* and *themselves*. Originally this dative usage was not confined to the 3rd person, as it now is: *me self* and *thee self* were common. M.E. examples are:

Orm. 12592 I *me sellf* sahh godess gast

K. Horn 45 And *þe selve* riȝt anon/Ne schaltu to dai henne gon.

With possessive pronoun. The fact that the possessive was
found originally only with the first and second persons
(*myself* and *thyself*) suggests the possibility that *my*
and *thy* were phonetic weakenings of the earlier datives
mē and *þē*, aided perhaps by analogy with *her* in *herself*
(accusative mistaken for genitive). *Myself* appears in
Layamon at the beginning of the 13th C; *thyself* in
Cursor Mundi at the beginning of the 14th C.:
Layam. 8816 Ah ich *mi seolf* neore & mine gode
cnihtes inumen weoren ure king.
Cursor M. 4604 Lok *thi selven* wit resun
By analogy this pseudo-genitive was extended to the
forms of the third person, *self* being regarded as a
substantive:
Cursor M. 15626 *His* hali *self* all suett.
Cursor M. 5378 To ches þam ware *þair-self* will neven
Both *hisself* and *theirselves* were in use in the early 19th
C, and are still found in dialect speech.

Despite the example from K. Alfred in (ii) above, the
regular use of the possessive *our* + *self* dates from M.E.
only. *Cursor Mundi* has *ur-selfe* and *ur-selven*; but *ourselves* occurs first in Tyndale's version of the Bible
(1525, reflexive use). Similarly *ȝurself* (reflex.) appears
first in *Cursor Mundi* and *youre selves* in Tyndale. Sweet
(*N.E.G.*, § 1109) thinks that the plurals in *-ves* were
formed on the analogy of nouns ending in *-lf*, like
shelf, *shelves*.

*Absolute use of myself, thyself, himself, herself, ourselves,
yourselves, themselves as emphatic subject*
The example from Alfred's *Orosius* in (iii) is clearly not
an example of the construction here dealt with. Most
grammarians agree that its earliest date is the 11th C.
The first example is with *him* + *self* and is found in the
Laws of Canute (c 1000):
§ 7 Nime him fîf . . . and beo *him sylf* sixta.

This omission of the personal pronoun subject was increased in M.E. and very popular in N.E. of the 16th and 17th
centuries. Examples abound in Shakespeare and Jonson.
In the 18th and 19th centuries it became a poetic archaism.

In Jonson and Shakespeare, in fact as late as Addison and Swift, the reflexive is printed as two words when the first element is a possessive pronoun, e.g. *my* self, *your* self, *our* selves. But *himself* and *herself* are generally printed as one word. This confirms the contention of the *N.E.D.* and many grammarians that *self* was in most of its uses regarded as substantival. Such expressions as 'your good *self*', 'Beauty's *self*' etc. support the view.

C.A. II. 1. 24 (125) Beggers will keepe fine,/Their daughters, being faire, though *themselves* pine

E.M.I.H. I. 1. 16 (197) *my selfe* was once a student

,, (F) II. 5. 14 (334) *our selves* were not the first

E.M.O.H. IV. 8. 66 (558) *your selfe* shall confesse nothing more possible

Revels V. 4. 333 (149) *themselves,* who beare the odours, have ever the least sence of them (= the very people)

Mag. La. Char. I. 60 (529) *Himselfe* hath done that

(b) Reflexive usages

In O.E., when the subject and object of a verb are the same person, i.e. when the action is reflected upon the doer, the object pronoun (now called reflexive) was merely the accusative of the subject personal pronoun. This usage is quite unbroken in the history of the language, though it has become archaic and poetical since the 18th C, e.g. When I lay *me* down to sleep.

Although *self* sometimes occurred after the object personal pronoun in O.E. and E.M.E., it seems merely to have emphasized it, not to have had any specific reflexive function. Some early examples (e.g. the second) have oblique cases after prepositions:

Will in Thorpe *Dipl. Angl.* (873) Ic wille ǣrist *mē siolfne* Gode allmehtȝum forȝēofan tō ðēre stowe æt Crīstes cirican.

Ags. Gosp. (c 1000), Mark III. 24. Gif his rice on *him sylfum* bið to-dǣled.

Aelfric, *Colloquy* (early 11th C) 240 Swāhwæðer þū sȳ . . . begā oþþe behwyrf *þe sylfne* on þisum

Ancren Riwle (c 1225) p. 124, þu dest me god, and hermest *þi sulf*

The historical source of the modern reflexive pronoun is almost certainly these ready-to-hand combinations of the personal pronoun + emphatic adjective. Those combinations that are now obsolete in the literary language are often preserved in the dialects (see Wright, *Dial. Gram.*, § 415).

The new construction proved a convenient means of avoiding ambiguity in the 3rd person, where reflexives, such as in 'He hurt *him*', could refer to another person. Nevertheless its spread was not rapid, for as late as Shakespeare and Jonson the old use of the personal pronoun outnumbers that of the new reflexive. The latter only became firmly established in the second half of the 17th C, when it ousted the former.

Uses of the personal pronoun as reflexive only have been recorded.

(i) *Personal pron. as reflexive (direct object)*

T.T. III. 9. 40 (58) He thus absents *him*, and dare not be seene

E.M.I.H. I. 2. 11 (203) hie *thee* in again (Franz *S.G.* § 307 regards *thee* after the imperative of certain intransitive verbs such as *haste, hie, get, go*, as a relict of an old dative. This seems very doubtful, even on the analogy of *Beowulf* 2388: *him* eft gewāt)

,, III. 1. 50 (234) Yet now I have bethought *me* to, I wil not (*bethought* is a regular reflexive verb; so is *beshrew* in the next example)

,, III. 2. 1 (238) Beshrew *me*

E.M.O.H. I. 1. 38 (443) I'le lay *me* downe

Revels I. 2. 81 (51) thou maiest dwell on earth, and sport *thee* there

Volp. I. 3. 28 (33) I feele *me* going

Cat. IV. 105 (501) Some cautions from his wife, how to behave *him*

N. Inn II. 6. 81 (438) Commit *you* to the steem !

(ii) *Reflexive personal pronoun as dative of advantage* (in good use in O.E.).

E.M.I.H. I. 1. 34 (198) I have bought *me* a hawk

Poet. II. 2. 21 (227) You have chosen *you* a most faire companion

Sej. II. 421 (389) doth make haste/To get *him* note, or name

Alch. III. 2. 46 (344) You cannot/ But raise *you* friends.

Note: There is a unique instance of *self* used absolutely, which, strangely enough, is the last example quoted in the *N.E.D.*

Volp. I. 2. 69 (30) Fooles, they are the onely nation . . ./Free from care, or sorrow-taking,/*Selves*, and others merry-making

Cf. Dickens, *Pickwick Papers*, Ch. xxxiv (end) "Well sir," said Dodson, for *self* and partner.

POSSESSIVE

24. Objective uses of the possessive pronoun

Like the possessive case of the noun, the possessive pronoun (the possessive case of the personal pronoun) is used with an objective meaning, i.e. a meaning which has a passive relation to the meaning of the word which the possessive pronoun qualifies. This objective use is still not uncommon in modern English, e.g. 'He said all he could in *my* defence', where *in my defence* means 'in defence of me'. But we generally prefer to denote it by means of the prepositional phrase, e.g. 'to prey on *their* remainder' would now be expressed by 'to prey on what remains *of them*'. In short, the objective use of the possessive pronoun is more frequent in E.N.E. than it is today.

E.M.I.H. IV. 3. 117 (266) shall I intreate so much favour of you for my friend as to direct and attend you to *his* meeting (= to meeting him)

,,　　(F) II. 5. 38 (335) To ruine of our states! Nay, when our owne/Portion is fled, to prey on *their* remainder (= the remainder of our states)

E.M.O.H. III. 9. 72 (525) I doe honour the meanest rush in this chamber for *your* love (= for love of you)

Revels V. 11. 127 (179) I was the authour, in some sort,/To worke *their* knowledge into Cynthia's sight (= knowledge of them)

Volp. IV. 5. 107 (102) Speake to the knave ?/ . . . my heart/Abhors *his* knowledge (= knowledge of him)

On the other hand, the possessive pronoun has sometimes in E.N.E. subjective meaning in phrases which would now be interpreted objectively, e.g.

Shakespeare *Tempest* V. 1. 119, Thy dukedom I resign, and do entreat/ Thou pardon me *my* wrongs, i.e. 'the wrongs I have done you' not 'the wrongs I have suffered'.

25. Use of 'my' between adjective and noun

In the form of address 'My Lord', still used in the courts of law, *my* is a term of respect. It has lost any possessive meaning which it may originally have had. Examples of the use occur in O.E., e.g. *Juliana* 166 Mīn sē swētesta sunnan scīma, Iuliana ! Bede *Ecc. Hist.* iii. 14 Hwæt woldest þū, *mīn* domne biscop.

This possessive of courtesy was inseparably bound to the governing noun, especially in the case of *mi lord*, which soon came to be written as one word (*cf.* French *monsieur*). Thus an adjective qualifying *lord* was placed before *my*, instead of between it and the noun, as in modern English. The usage was then extended to other substantives, e.g. Shakespeare *L.L.L.* I. 2. 63, Sweete *my* child. This order is found as late as the 17th Century.

N. Inn III. 2. 146 (456) Nay, sweet *my* Lord, I must appeale the Soveraigne

26. Indefinite use of 2nd pers. possessive pronoun 'your', largely to denote familiarity

In its origin this indefinite use of *your* probably bears some relation to the ethic dative. It does not go so far back, however, the first occurrence recorded in the *N.E.D.* being in Ascham's *Scholemaster* (1568). It has no possessive function, but seems rather to be deliberative and judicial, assuming an attitude of familiarity with the subject on the part both of the speaker and the person addressed. In many contexts *your* denotes familiarity bordering on contempt; but Abbott's view (*S.G.* § 221) that it indicates vulgarity or rudeness in the speaker is based on a few examples only.

In some of its uses *your* resembles the Lat. *iste*; in others the interpolative *putes* (= you would think). It was still found fairly commonly in the 19th C, but is now obsolescent.

E.M.I.H. II. 3. 77 (228) it's *your* only best humor sir, *your* true melancholy

E.M.O.H. I. 2. 6 (444) I am like *your* taylors needle, I goe through

,, III. 3. 30 (500) *your* onely admiration is *your* silence

Alch. IV. 4. 7-10 (372) Aske from *your* courtier, to *your* innes of courtman,/To *your* mere millaner: they will tell you all,/*Your* Spanish iennet is the best horse, etc.

Stap. N. I. 2. 110 (289) thence comes *your* proverbe;/The Taylor makes the man.

Mag. La. II. 6. 92 (541) Seventhly, *your* wise poore men/Have ever beene contented to observe/Rich Fooles

27. Use of possessive pronoun with numerals in a distributive sense

The *N.E.D.* has the following example from Lord Eldon (1827): 'A sportsman was thought nothing of unless he could kill *his* thousand birds a day'. This appears with other examples under sub-head 2. b. of *his*, and is described as the use "with objects which are not one's property, but which one ought to have, or has specially to deal with . . . or which are the common possession of a class in which everyone is assumed to have his share". The last of these suggestions covers the use here cited; it may be called the distributive possessive, and is still occasionally found.

E.M.I.H. IV. 2. 80 (261) every man, *his* twentie a day

Volp. II. 2. 62 (51) These . . . rogues . . . are able, very well, to kill *their* twentie a weeke

28. Pleonastic use of possessive pronoun before gerund

In modern English the possessive pronoun is called into use before the verbal noun in -*ing* only when it is necessary to indicate the agent of the action or to avoid confusion of the latter with some other person mentioned in the sentence. In all other circumstances it is regarded as pleonastic and omitted. An example of this pleonastic use is given by Fowler (*Modern English Usage* p. 216): Sure as she was of *her* never losing her filial hold of the beloved. This limitation of the possessive pronoun before a gerund is not found in E.N.E.

E.M.O.H. V. 6. 15 (582) hee'ld bee content . . . to pay him five for one, at *his* next meeting him in Paules

Cat. I. 107 (438) when Orestilla, by *her* bearing well/These my retirements, and stolne times for thought,/Shall give their effects leave to call her Queene

29. Possessive as antecedent of a relative pronoun

The relative qualifies the possessive instead of the substantive nearest it. The possessive is generally a pronoun; but often the same construction occurs with a noun. Shakespeare and Jonson employed it frequently, both in verse and prose.

In O.E. the possessive case of the demonstrative *sē, sēo, þæt* could be used as antecedent to the commonest relative *þe,* e.g.

Cura Pastoralis 16: Ðonne se scrift ongit ðæs costunga ðe hē him ondetteþ.

But the possessive personal pronoun as antecedent does not seem to occur in O.E.—there is no example in Bosworth and Toller or the *N.E.D.* The latter is found first in M.E. with the relative *that,* which took over the function of *þe* and, like it, was used for all genders, e.g.

Chaucer, *Second Nun's Tale* 138, And for *his* love *that* deyde upon a tree.

A possible explanation of the M.E. usage is that the possessive was looked upon simply as a personal pronoun in the genitive case, and therefore grammatically correct as antecedent. But this makes the lack of the construction in O.E. the more curious.

In modern English the construction is avoided because the genitive possessive before a noun is adjectival in function, and usage requires a substantive or pronoun as antecedent of the relative. The genitive substitute (*of* with the accusative of the personal pronoun) is therefore favoured.

The possessive as antecedent of the relative pronoun is still permissible in poetry, and is encountered in prose of the 19th C and even later:

e.g. Scott, *Ivanhoe*: more shame to *their* folly, who have suffered thee
      to grow grey in usury
  Wilde, *Intentions*, in *his* soul who wrought it.
E.M.I.H. III. 4. 63 (249) Then shouldst thou be *his* prisoner, *who* is
    thine
E.M.O.H. III. 4. 110 (506) Spread your selfe upon *his* bosome publikely
    whose heart you would eate in private
Revels V. 5. 21 (159) And at *her* sight, turnes forth-with regular,/
    Whose scepter guides the flowing ocean
Sej. V. 240 (445) Yet, why is, now, *my* thought turn'd toward death,/
    Whom fates have let goe on, so farre, in breath
Volp. IV. 5. 61 (101) So much more full of danger is *his* vice,/*That* can
    beguile so
Cat. IV. 5. (498) That we might laugh at *their* ridiculous feare,/*Whose*
    names we trembled at
Mag. La. Chor. IV. 10 (578) *our* parts *that* are the Spectators . . . are
    to await the processe

    Note: With substantival possessive:
E.M.I.H. I. 1. 124 (200) What might the *gentlemans* name be, sir, *that*
    sent it ?

30. Possessive pronoun between demonstrative and noun

The old construction *this my friend* is found alongside of the newer and now regular *this friend of mine* in the 16th and 17th centuries. Franz (*S.G.* § 331) says the former is the more frequent in Shakespeare.

The demonstrative pronoun before the possessive is determinative; it dates from O.E., e.g. Matthew XXV. 40 Ānum of *þysum mīnum* lǣstum gebrōðrum.

E.M.O.H. II. 3. 109-10 (472) *this my* house stood on the Muses hill
Cat. I. 107 (438) *These my* retirements and stolne times for thought.
Cf. Shakespeare *Merry Wives* IV. 2. 23 seemed but tameness, civility,
    and patience, to *this his* distemper he is in now:

31. Absolute possessives

The absolute possessive was in use in O.E., e.g. John XVII. 10 Ealle *mīne* synd *þīne* and *þīne* synd *mīne; O.E. Chronicle* (A.D. 1016), hergodon hī on heora healfe, ond Cnut on *his*.

(a) Introduction of intrusive final -s

In M.E. all the possessives which in O.E. ended in *-re* (now *-r*), when used absolutely, added an *-s*, e.g. *heres, oures, youres*. This practice apparently first occurred in the late 13th C, e.g. *Havelock the Dane*, 2801, For Englond aughte forto ben *Youres*, and we youre men.

The *-s* was also added to the Norse borrowing *þeȝȝre* (*their*). It was a Northern ending. The Southern and Midland dialects considerably later (mid 14th C) took *-n*, e.g. *hern, ourn, yourn*.

The *-s* ending was also added occasionally to other possessive pronouns, one surviving in the modern Scots form *mines*, e.g. Stevenson, *Catriona*, neither your affair nor *mine's*.

The old possessive absolute (without intrusive *-s*) existed alongside of the new, however, until the 17th C, e.g. Fletcher, *Fair Maid* II. 1, This affront of *your*.

The origin of the final *-s* is variously accounted for. Sweet (*N.E.G.* I. 1096) says that it is an extension of the *-s* of *his*. The *N.E.D.* (see under *Hers*) suggests that it arose by association with the *-s* appended to the post-possessive in the construction 'a horse *of the kinges*', which is in effect a double possessive.[1]

The fact that the absolute possessives *heres, oures, youres,* occur only a little before this post-possessive 'a horse of the kinges' suggests that the *N.E.D.*'s explanation is quite likely. But direct evidence that the latter construction occurred as early as the 13th C would have to be adduced (see footnote).

C.A. II. I. 48 (126) Here have I chang'd my forme, my name and *hers*

„ II. 7. 32 (136) And how are their plaies ? as *ours* are ?

---

[1] Den Breejen (*Genitive and its of- equivalent*, ch. XI, p. 142) says that the construction 'a horse of the kings' is very old, and that its beginnings are to be found in O.E.; but he gives no examples from that period. The uses in M.E., which date from the beginning of 14th C., show that it only occurs with nouns denoting persons and proper names.

(b) One noun determined by two possessives, the first of which is absolute (used elliptically)

In modern English the absolute possessive usually stands last, e.g. There is no difference between your house and *mine*. In the examples here listed the order is reversed, e.g. There is no difference between *yours* and my house. The former dates from O.E., but I have been unable to discover an example of the latter before the 16th C.

Note: In O.E. both possessives could also be placed after the substantive, e.g. *Psalm* LIV. 13 On godes hūse gangan swylce mid geþeahtunge *þine* and *mine*.

Fowler (*M.E.U.* p. 6) condemns the absolute possessive in the first position, e.g. Shakespeare *Tempest* II. 1. 245 In *yours* and my discharge, and Byron, *Manfred* II. 4. 33. What, know'st thou not/*Thine* and our Sovereign? He requires in modern English *your* and *thy* respectively. Nevertheless numerous instances of the absolute possessive first, occur as late as the 19th C, even in prose (see examples quoted by Jespersen, *Modern English Grammar* II. 16. 25). The usage is rare in Jonson.

Cat. III. 240 (476) When both thy Senate, and thy gods doe sleepe,/
And neither *thine*, nor their own states doe keepe !

,, IV. 1. (498) Can these men feare? Who are not onely *ours*,/
But the worlds masters ?

(c) The usage 'of + possessive absolute'

A good deal of discussion has centred round the origin of the type-expression 'a friend *of mine*' and its noun equivalent 'a friend *of the king's*'. Various theories have been put forward by Maetzner (*E.G.* III, p. 222), Kellner (*H.O.E.S.* §§ 178-80), Einenkel (*Anglia* 33), W. v. d. Gaaf (*Neophilologus*, XII), Den Breejen (*Genitive and its of-equivalent*, ch. XI), Jespersen (*M.E.G.* III. 1. 5), the most explicit being the last. Kellner calls the usage a pseudopartitive genitive.

Though it may have arisen as a partitive genitive (see *N.E.D.* under *Of* XIII. 44), its use has certainly been extended. It is, according to Jespersen, no longer a partitive, but an appositional genitive; he compares it with the Latin genitive of description. "*Of* in all these cases", he says, "may be said to be simply a grammatical device to make it possible to join words which it is for some reason or other difficult or impossible to join immediately . . . if we want to assign a definite meaning to this *of*, we may say that it means 'who is' or 'which is'." A friend *of* mine = a friend *who is* mine.

The use of *of* + absolute genitive dates from the early 14th C. It seems to occur first in the *Cursor Mundi* and is common in Chaucer.

T.T. III. 5. 5 (49) Here is a strange thing, call'd a Lady, a Mad-dame:/And a device *of hers* yclept her woman
E.M.I.H. I. 3. 181 (211) a friend *of mine* told me so
Revels I. 1. 63 (46) you borrowed a girdle *of hers*
Stap. N. V. 1. 8 (365) Why doe not all that are of those societies,/Come forth, and gratulate me one *of theirs* ?

(*d*) *Demonstrative + noun + 'of' with possessive absolute*
The construction *this friend of mine* (not found before the 15th C) appeared alongside, and finally took the place of, the construction *this my friend* mentioned in the last section. It occurs earliest in Malory's *Morte D'Arthur* and Caxton's translation of *Blanchardyn and Eglantine*. Kellner (*H.O. E.S.* § 178) notes that in many combinations of this type no idea of partition is included; e.g. in 'that beautiful face *of hers*' we could not read *of her faces*. The construction cannot then be designated a partitive genitive, as originally suggested.

Jespersen's idea that the preposition *of* has the significance of 'which is' again applies, though the origin is not explained. Abbott (*S.G.* § 239) likens the construction to the Latin use of *iste*, *of* + absolute genitive being purely adjectival in function.

E.M.I.H. I. 4. 129 (217) *that* huge tumbrell slop *of yours*
Volp. III. 3. 15 (70) *this* feat body *of mine* doth not crave/Halfe the meat

32. Idiomatic and metrical use of 'of' with personal pronoun
The preposition *of*, followed by the first personal pronoun in the objective case, is used by Jonson, as by other writers, for different idiomatic purposes. Shakespeare has it also with the

third person, e.g. *Henry IV*, Part I, II. 1. 12 it was the death
of him. An analysis of the examples below shows that *of me*
is not always equivalent to *my*. Thus, in modern English
'You'll be the death of me', which resembles the Shakespeare
example just quoted, the meaning is 'you will cause my death',
and not 'you will be my death'. The use of the prepositional
combination may, therefore, connote causation.

Jonson's uses seem to fall into four categories, the last of which
is plainly metrical or to meet the requirements of rhyme.

(*a*) *Periphrastic 'of me' (= my) in a sentimental sense*
    This periphrasis has been common in popular speech and
    poetry from E.N.E. times, e.g. Herrick, *To Anthea*

> Thou art my life, my love, my heart,
> The very eyes *of me*.

D. H. Lawrence uses it with intentional sentimentality in
Softly in the dusk a woman is singing to me: Till the heart
of me weeps to belong/To the old Sunday evenings at home.

E.M.I.H. I. 3. 76. (208) By the body *of me* (Expletive, used by Cob)

(*b*) *Use after 'never (not) a'*
    Here *my* cannot be substituted for idiomatic *of me*. The
    semantic equivalent seems to be 'not a single one of my'.

E.M.I.H. III. 4. 103 (250) I can hold *never a* bone *of me* still (The
    speaker is Giuliano; there is reason to believe that the ex-
    pression is bucolic).

(*c*) *Use of 'of me' for modern 'of mine'*
    The following construction should be compared with (*d*)
    of the last section.

E.M.O.H. V. 7. 40 (586) Was't not a good device this same *of me*,
    sirs

(*d*) *Metrical use*
    The following use, which occurs in a ballad, is sportive and
    emphatic, and is used for the sake of rhyme:

Masque of Augurs 176 (635) We came from St. Katharin-a;/These
    dancing three,/By the helpe *of mee*,/Who am the Post of the
    signe-a.

51

DEMONSTRATIVE

For the sake of convenience the demonstrative adjective is here treated with the demonstrative pronoun.

33. 'This' with periods of time in the plural

Examples occur in many other writers, e.g. Shakespeare, *Rom. and Jul.* V. 2. 25 Within *this* three houres will faire Iuliet wake. The *N.E.D.* has an instance as late as 1883: L. Oliphant *Altiora Peto* II. 261, *This* last six months. An explanation frequently offered is that *this* is a weakening of the L.M.E. plural *þise.* The history of the latter form is briefly as follows:—

In E.M.E. masc. *þĕs* and fem. *þēos* fell together as *þēs*, with neuter *þis.* Later, two plural forms with adjectival inflexion *-e, þēse* and *þise*, took the place of the O.E. common plural *þās*, which in E.M.E. came to be used alongside of, and may have been confused with, *þā* plural of *þat* (O.E. *þæt*), giving the latter the N.E. plural *those.* N.E. *these* is from L.M.E. *þēse.* Both *þise* and *þēse* occur in Malory's *Morte D'Arthur*, and both plurals passed into E.N.E.

The explanation that the period of time, even in M.E., was regarded as what Jespersen calls a 'unified plural' (see *M.E.G.* II, ch. v) is, however, equally valid and, on the whole, more probable.[1] For instance, Mandeville has *'this* thre dayes', where *this* is probably singular; and Chaucer writes in *The Book of the Duchesse*, 37: a siknesse/That I have suffred *this* eight yere. This explanation certainly applies to 19th C examples like that cited from L. Oliphant in the *N.E.D.* Moreover, plurals occur after other words in the singular, notably *that*, e.g. Chaucer, *Romaunt of Rose* 990, *that* other fyve.

Examples in Jonson show both singular and plural forms, though the singular demonstrative is rare:

(*a*) E.M.I.H. II. 1. 57 (221) any time *this* xiiij yeares
(*b*) Epic. I. 1. 142 (168) *Tru.* . . . When saw you Dauphine Eugenie ?
 Cle. Not *these* three daies.

34. Idiomatic use of 'this' for 'the' in 'this other day'

The unexplained use of the near-demonstrative *this* in the above phrase is not comparable to the use of *that* in 'that other day', where *that* is a relict of the old definite article. As the

---

[1] But cf. Shakespeare *Henry VIII*, III. 2. 360, *This* many summers in a sea of glory, where the explanation of the lost inflexional *-e* seems more likely.

usage, which dates from 1300 to 1600 only, occurs with no other adverbial phrase of time than the stereotyped 'other day', 'þæt oþer dæg' may have influenced it.

The classified division of examples in the *N.E.D.* (see under *Other* A. 3. b.) suggests that 'this other day', like 'the other day', referred at first to the immediate past (i.e. the preceding day, yesterday; cf. *this* morning, when it refers not to the present, but to the immediate past). Later its use was extended to mean 'a few days ago'.

Historical instances from the *N.E.D.* precede the single example from Jonson.

c. 1300 *Cursor Mundi* 5672 Wil þu me sla as þu did an, þis oder day
1421 Hoccleve, *Complaint* 309 *This* othar day a lamentacion/Of a wofull man in a boke I sye
1596 Shakespeare, *Henry IV*, Part I, III. 3. 152 He ... sayde *this* other day,/You ought him a thousand pound (Franz, *S.G.* § 316 (*d*) gives three other examples from Shakespeare)
E.M.I.H. I. 3. 157 (211) *this* other day I hapned to enter into some discourse of a hanger

35. Original use of 'this' with the word 'present', where modern English has the definite article

Examples in the *N.E.D.* (see under *Present* I. 2) show that *this present* dates from E.N.E., and disappeared from use during the 17th C. The definite article in 'the present' then became emphatic as *this* had been. *N.E.D.* suggests, as possible origin of the latter, analogy with O.F., e.g. *ceste* present chartre.

E.M.I.H. (F) III. 3. 63 (348) The manner he hath stood with, till *this* present,/Doth promise no such change !
Sej. III. 501 (435) Seianus brest/Never receiv'd more full contentments in, /Then at *this* present.

36. Idiomatic 'this' (= now)

As early as O.E. neuter *þis* and *þæt* were used after the prepositions *ǽr*, *æfter* and *ōþ* as adverbial phrases of time, e.g. Exodus II. 1, Æfter *þisum* fōr ān esne of Levies hīwrǽdene and nam wīf on his āgenum cynne.

In M.E. various other prepositions were employed with *this* in the same way, and the usage has continued in certain idiomatic phrases until the present day, e.g. Keats, *Endymion* I, 988 By *this* the sun is setting (= by this time).
E.M.I.H. I. 3. 51 (208) I should have carried two turnes by *this*.

37. Emphatic use of 'that' to avoid repetition of preceding word, phrase or clause

In this idiomatic usage *that* is generally preceded by the conjunction *and*; sometimes *but* occurs. The origin of the idiom is probably to be found in the desire to avoid repetition of a preceding word, phrase, or clause, to which *that* always refers. An instance occurs in L.O.E., e.g. c. 1000. *Saxon Leechdoms* I. 278. On þām (berries) ys sǣd and *þæt* sweart. Chaucer has (*Friar's Tale* 294) I have been syk and *that* ful many a day (examples from *N.E.D.*, *That* B. I. 2. a). In the latter example *that* refers to *I have been syk*.

Though instances are to be found in the 19th C, the usage appears to be obsolescent.

E.M.I.H. I. 4. 138 (217) he shall heare on't, and *that* tightly too

> *Note*: Another emphatic use of *that*, with the numeral *one*, meaning 'a single', occurs in Jonson. It is a nonce use, and may have been employed for metrical reasons:
> Sej. V. 81 (439) I know not *that* one deity, but Fortune;/To whom, I would throw up . . ./One grane of incense

38. Idiomatic use of 'that' followed by relative conjunctions 'that' and 'as'

The use of the demonstrative adjective here is emphatic, indicating at the same time degree or kind. The construction, which occurs with following correlative *that* or *as*, dates from E.N.E. and was still in good use in the early 19th C, e.g.

Shelley in *Lady S. Mem.* (1859) 155, I hope that I have treated the question with *that* temper and spirit *as* to silence cavil

Dickens, *Dombey and Son*, XLVII, He . . . struck her . . . with *that* heaviness, *that* she tottered on the marble floor.

The *N.E.D.* considers that the construction is now archaic or dialectal.

For Franz (*S.G.* § 340 (*c*)) the main interest is in the use of *as* as a relative pronoun, which dates from the 12th C (O.E. *ealswā*, E.M.E. *alse*). *As* was first used in this function after *such* and *same*.

(*a*) E.M.O.H. III. 9. 39 (524) She do's dart them abroad with *that* sweete loose, and iudiciall aime, *that* you would . . .

    cf. Shakespeare *Hamlet* I. 5. 48. From me whose love was of *that* dignity/*That* it went hand in hand even with the vow/I made to her in marriage.

(b) E.M.I.H. I. 4. 156-7 (217) not reposed in *that* securitie,/*As* I could wish

    E.M.O.H. V. 2. 24 (567) a gentleman . . . of *that* rare and admirable facultie, *as* . . . I know not his like in Europe.

    Revels I. 5. 62 (63) We act our mimicke trickes with *that* free licence, . . ./*As* if we practiz'd in a paste-board case

    Cf. Shakespeare *Jul. Cæsar* I. 2. 33. I have not from your eyes *that* gentleness/*As* I was wont to have.

39. Idiomatic use of 'here' (= this) and 'there' (= that)

According to the *N.E.D.* this falls under different categories:—

(a) Use mainly with verb 'to be', indicating something present or offered.

    E.M.I.H. V. 3. 271 (283) *Theres* for you sir

    Mag. La. IV. 7. 29 (574) She shall pretend,/T'have had a fit o' the Mother: *there* is all.

    Cf. Shakespeare *Twelf. N.* IV. 1. 27 Now sir, have I met you again: *ther's* for you.

(b) To point out some person or thing with approval or dis-approval. The notion of place is also present. *Cf.* modern English '*there's* a good fellow'.

    E.M.O.H. V. 2. 117 (570) looke you, ladie, what a palme *here* is

    Revels I. 1. 21 (44) Daring ? O Ianus ! what a word is *there* ?

    Cf. Shakespeare *Tam. Shrew* V. 2. 180 Why *there's* a wench: Come on and kisse mee Kate.

40. 'Here' or 'there' + preposition, instead of preposition + demonstrative 'this' or 'that'

Parallel constructions occur in O.E. and E.M.E., e.g.

Beowulf 118: Fand þā ðǣr inne æþelinga gedriht/swefan æfter symble (the reference is to *hêan hûses* in 116)

Aelfric, *Colloquy*, 75: Hundas bedrifon hyne tō mē, and ic þǣr togaēnes standende fǣrlīce ofstikode hyne

Owl and Nightingale: *Her among* nis no chateringe (the reference is to a boast made by the Nightingale about her song in the previous sentence).

In L.O.E. combinations such as *hereof, herewith, hereon,* were common. The most likely explanation is that formations of this type arose through the juxtaposition of two adverbs. In English many adverbs are, however, also prepositions. It is possible that by L.M.E. or E.N.E. the second adverb was looked upon as a preposition governing the preceding *here* or *there,* as if the latter were actually a demonstrative pronoun, and that this led to many analogous formations.

Except in the case of *therefore*, these combinations are now regarded as archaic. They are retained, however, in official language and some correspondence (especially in South African English usage).

E.M.O.H. Induc. 199 (435) *therein* I commend your carefull thoughts
    ,,   I. 3. 127 (456) with the straw *thereof*/I'le stuffe the out-sides

41. Omission of demonstrative antecedent after 'there are' etc.

The unemphatic initial use of *ðǣr* (= there), with inverted order of the subject, in order to prepare the reader or listener for a subject which is to be specially emphasized, dates from O.E. There is considerable loss of the place sense, e.g.

Beowulf 271 ne sceal *þǣr* dyrne sum wesan, þæs ic wēne.
K. Alfred, *Boethius* III. 1 Þā cōm *þǣr* gān in tō mē heofencund Wīsdōm.

The *N.E.D.* (see *There* B. 1. 4) points out that, before the verb 'to be' or auxiliary verbs, *there* has a slight stress, whereas before notional verbs it is unstressed.

When the subject, meaning 'a certain kind of people', was the antecedent of a following relative clause, the generic demonstrative (usually plural, *those*) was originally omitted, and the emphasis was apparently shifted to the subject of the relative clause. The *N.E.D.* suggests that it may be a Latinism, based on such sentences as 'sunt qui dicunt'. Examples date from the beginning of the 15th C only; the construction was obsolescent in the 17th C, being used later only after *there are*, and probably as a conscious archaism (see *N.E.D.*, *There* B. 1. 4. f).

Poet. III. 5. 1 (257) There are, to whom I seeme excessive sower;
Volp. Ded. 65 (18) there are, that professe to have a key for the de-
cyphering of every thing:

42. Use of 'same' to strengthen demonstrative

The redundant use of *same* after a demonstrative is plainly emphatic and colloquial. It originated about the middle of the 14th C, was common in writers like Malory in the 15th, but reached the height of its popularity in the drama and other colloquial literature of the 16th and 17th centuries. The *N.E.D.* points out (i) that, of the 95 uses of *same* in Shakespeare, 55 are after a demonstrative; (ii) that the evidence is that the pleonastic word suggests playful familiarity, or a slight degree of annoyance or contempt.

Since the early 19th C this emphatic use of *same* has been regarded as a vulgarism. In Cockney and other dialects of England the adverb *here* (e.g. *this here* dog) has practically supplanted it.

In Jonson's *Every Man in His Humour* 'this same' is constantly on the lips of characters like *Cob*, who spoke the Cockney of their day.

E.M.I.H. I. 3. 67 (208) reading of *these same* abominable, . . . verses
  ,, I. 4. 10 (213) did you see *that same* fellow there ?
E.M.O.H. I. 3. 88 (455) Who brought *this same*, sirha ?
Volp. IV. 2. 7 (94) *That same's* the party ! In mans apparell.
Alch. III. 4. 147 (355) *Dap.* I have some Philip, and Maries. *Fac.* I, *those same*/Are best of all.
Cat. IV. 613 (517) What is *that same* Umbrenus, was the agent ?
D.A. I. 4. 92 (175) 'Twas prettily said, *that same*
Mag. La. V. 10.79 (593) Good faith, *this same* is like to turne a busines.

RELATIVE AND INTERROGATIVE

A. THE WH- PRONOUNS

The O.E. *hw-* pronouns (later *wh-*) were all originally interrogative. They came to be used as relatives in various ways and at different times.

43. N.E. relative use of 'who'[1] for things

Who, though used by Jonson frequently, is not mentioned as a relative in his *Grammar*, *which* being given as the general relative.

In O.E. the interrogatives *hwā* and *hwilc* had a different connotation. *Hwilc* was definite and selective, *hwā* general; *hwilc* (originally only an adjective) could be used both as an adjective and a noun, *hwā* only as a noun. The interrogative use of *hwā*, *hwæs* for things is found in O.E., e.g. *Crist.* 1199, *Hwæs* wēneð sē þe mid gewitte . . .

---

[1] O.E. interrogative *hwā* had, as oblique cases, acc. *hwone*, gen. *hwæs*, dat. *hwǣm* or *hwām*. The last of these forms was used as the direct object (of the indefinite relative) as early as the 12th C. The relative use of the gen. *whose* also dates from the 12th C. The N.E. nom. *who* appeared as a relative compounded with *that* early in the 13th C, but not by itself until the end of that century, and was not then much used until the 16th C.

The relative use of *who* (genit. *whose*) for things is quite frequent in the late 16th and early 17th centuries. The *N.E.D.* and many historical grammars seem to confine the relative *who* for things to (*a*) use with animals, (*b*) use for the purposes of personification. Examples are produced in the *N.E.D.* from the late 16th and succeeding centuries only. But there are many examples in Shakespeare which do not appear to fit into these two categories (see Franz *S.G.* § 335 (*a*)), e.g. *Merch. Ven.* II. 7. 5 (casket scene) The first of gold, *who* this inscription bears. There are, moreover, earlier examples, for instance in Chaucer's *Rom. of Rose* 4194: Men seyn over the walle stonde/Grete engynes, *who* were nigh honde (amended by Skeat to *which*).

The likeliest explanation seems to be that *who*, when it first came to be used as a relative pronoun, had common gender; but that during the Elizabethan period it was limited to persons (or to things personified). In 1621 Gill (*Logonomia Anglica* ch. VI) gives *whü* as only masculine or feminine, but *which* as of all genders. Butler in his *English Grammar* (1634) ch. III, supports Gill in restricting *who* (relative and interrogative) to persons and applying *which* to all genders.

Both in the nominative and oblique cases of the relative, Jonson employs *who* for *which* mainly where personification is intended. In the example from Sejanus under (*a*) below, the idea of personification is, however, extremely weak, probably doubtful.

Whose for *of which* is still commonly used for things, especially where *of which* is felt to be syntactically clumsy.

(*a*) *Nominative*

T.T. III. 9. 57 (58) At the report of it, an *Oxe* did speake;/*Who* dy'd soone after (*who* with animals is very common in writers of this period).

T.T. V. 10. 66 (91) The *Lawes, who* have a noose to crack his neck,/ As Iustice Bramble tells him

E.M.O.H. IV. 6. 144 (551) the evill *angels* that she gave him, *who* have indeed tempted the simple youth (angels = coins)

Sej. IV. 70 (420) a fortune sent to exercise/Your vertue, as the wind doth trie strong *trees*:/*Who* by vexation grow more sound, and firme

Alch. Ded. 17 (290) lest it ... looke like one of the ambitious *Faces* of the time: *who*, the more they paint, are the lesse themselves
„ II. 3. 154 (326) It turnes to *sulphur*, or to *quick-silver*:/ *Who* are the parents of all other mettalls.

(b) *Genitive*

E.M.I.H. I. 1. 72-3 (199) and you be left like an unsavorie *snuffe,/*
Whose propertie is onely to offend.

E.M.O.H. IV. 2. 79 (533) feed that *life, whose* head hangs so heavily

Sej. IV. 119 (422) forsake/The *place, whose* glories warm'd you.

44. Relative[1] 'which' preceded by definite article

Examples, though rare, occur in O.E.:

e.g. *Lindis. Gosp.* Mark XV. 6. ān of þǣm gebundenum, þone
suœ *huœlcne* hia gigiuudon.

Probably what is meant is 'the whomsoever' or 'him whomsoever'; Latin, *unum ex vinctis, quemcumque petissent.* Author.
Version, *one prisoner, whomsoever they desired.*

This is not noted in the *N.E.D.*, which records the first examples from *Cursor Mundi* at the beginning of the 14th C. *The
which* was, in fact, not much used until M.E., when its frequent
employment must have been due, as Sweet suggested (*N.E.G.*
II. § 2132), to the influence of French *lequel.* The compound
is used adjectivally and pronominally, and both for persons and
things, though mainly for the latter. In French *lequel, laquelle,*
is used only as a relative pronoun, and chiefly in the following
circumstances:

(a) When the relative pronoun, referring to a thing, is preceded
by a preposition, or the words *parmi* or *entre.*

(b) To avoid ambiguity in cases where the relative is separated
from its antecedent.

Similar uses occur in M.E. and E.N.E. Though syntactically
the which has no function different from *which* in N.E., it seems
to be called into use (a) as an archaism (b) for the sake of emphasis
or clarity, or (c) as a metrical device for securing an extra
syllable.

Examples in the *N.E.D.* show that *the which* was employed
as late as the 19th C.

Shakespeare has a single example of *the whom*, which is not
found in Jonson, viz. *Winter's Tale* IV. 4. 520 you may/Enjoy

---

[1] There is a nonce use in Jonson of *the which* in interrogative function e.g.
Entertainment at Blackfriars 142 (773), But what is this to us, Mrs. Holdback ?
the which is the better nurse, the wet or the drye ? (prose).

That this use is rare is shown by the fact that the *N.E.D.* has only one example in a dependent clause (see under *which* B.I. 3. b), and that example occurs
in M.E.

your mistress, from *the whom*, I see,/There's no disjunction to be made.

E.M.O.H. II. 2. 10 (466) I will step forward three pases: of *the which*, I will barely retire one (Prose. Used by Puntarvolo in the language of chivalry—a conscious medievalism)

Sej. III. 410 (406) yet those words/Not reaching eyther prince, or princes parent:/*The which* your law of treason comprehends. (Metrical device)

D.A. I. 1. 87 (167) then this your grave choice/Might have done that, with his Lord Chefe, *the which*/Most of his chamber can doe now (Metrical device. The relative is also separated from the antecedent)

45. 'What' (a) as interrogative pronoun with persons (= who) (b) as interrogative adverb meaning 'why' or 'how'

(*a*) O.E. *hwæt* was the neuter of *hwā*, and thus from its inception was used for inanimate things. But predicatively *hwæt* was used with persons very early. Both the *N.E.D.* (see *what* A. I. 2) and Bosworth and Toller seem to find their earliest examples from L.O.E.; e.g.

Aelfric's translation of the Heptateuch: Gen. 27. 32 Đā cwæþ Isaac: *Hwæt* eart ðū ? Hē andwirde: Ic eom Esau. In *Beowulf* 233: hine fyrwyt bræc/mōdgehygdum, *hwæt* þā men wǣron, the meaning is probably 'of what race or sort'.

Until the close of the 17th C this predicative usage of the neuter interrogative pronoun *what* was common when the inquiry had reference to the name or identity of the person. In modern English *who* is preferred here, and *what* is restricted to ascertaining character, nature, function or office.

The use of *what* predicatively for persons should be compared with the similar use of *it* and *that*. Jespersen (*Phil. of Gram.* p. 242) says there is a universal tendency in language to make predicatives neuter.

Many examples of *what* for *who* in Jonson, as in Shakespeare, are extremely doubtful. Often the meaning is nearer to 'what sort of person', as in the example from *Beowulf* quoted above.

E.M.I.H. III. 2. 45 (239) Doctor Clement, *what's* he ?

Revels I. 4. 36 (55) Crites, you may say to him, *what* I am, if you please.

Cf. Shakespeare, *Othello* I. 1. 95 *what* are you? *Rod.* my name is Roderigo.

(b) (i) *Hwæt* as the interrogative adverb of reason occurs in
O.E. in Alfred's *Boethius* XIV, § 2 (late 9th C): *Hwæt*
murcnast þū þonn æfter þām þē þū forlure ?   This use
of *what* is found as late as the 17th C.   Analogy with the
similar use of *quid* in Latin is a possible origin.

E.M.I.H. III. 3. 40 (244) Spite of the Devill, *what* do I stay here
then ?
cf. Shakespeare, *Jul. Caesar* II. 1. 123 *What* need we any spur
but our own cause ?
It seems that the use of *what* for *why* is very common
before *need*.

(ii) *What* as the interrogative adverb of manner or degree
is first found in the *Ormulum*; it occurs as late as Tennyson and Ruskin.   Analysis of the examples in the *N.E.D.*
shows that *what* is used instead of 'how' or 'to what
extent' mainly before the verbs *avail*, *matter* or *signify*,
or before *the* + a comparative.

Revels V. 4. 324 (149) *what* are you the better ?
cf. Shakespeare, *Ven. and Adon.* 207 *What* were thy lips the
worse for one poor kiss ?

46. Use of interrogative 'whether' (= which of the two)

O.E. *hwæþer* was used adjectivally in the 9th C; but the
N.E.D. has no pronominal use until the end of the O.E. period.
Jonson has only one instance, in the Northern dialect of *The
Sad Shepherd*; it introduces a disjunctive dependent question,
after the verb *doubt*.   Wright's *Dialect Dictionary* shows that
the pronoun is still found in the Northern dialects of England.

S.S. II. 1. 20 (27) her sel' had doubted/*Whether* had been the liker of
the twa ! (Here *whether* = *which*.   The speaker is Maudlin)

Shakespeare has a similar use of *whether* in a direct question:

Merry Wives III. 2. 2. *Whether* had you rather lead mine eyes, or eye
your master's heels ?

47. Continuative use of wh- relatives, where modern English uses 'and + demonstrative'

In modern English the relative *which* is not, except in special
circumstances, used after a longer pause than a comma.   Conjunctival uses such as those illustrated below, if found at all,
are clearly archaisms; their frequency in E.N.E., both in attri-

butive and pronominal situations, is probably to be ascribed to the connecting use of *qui* in Latin constructions.

E.M.I.H. II. 2. 5 (222) How to reduce him from affected will/To reasons manage; *which* while I intend

Revels IV. 3. 297 (118) bequeath'd to mee this glove; *which* golden legacie, the Emperour himselfe tooke care to send after me.

Sej. III. 204 (399) custome hath allow'd/The magistrate, to call forth private men;/And to appoint their day: *which* priviledge/We may not in the Consul see infring'd

Volp. I. 4. 112 (39) *Corb.* Mine owne proiect. *Mos. Which* when he hath done, Sir—

Mag. La. III. 6. 90 (559) *Com.* . . . Only one vertue, they call Fortitude,/ Worthy the name of valour. *Iro. Which*, who hath not,/Is justly thought a Coward:

48. Relative use of adverb 'where' (+ preposition) in place of the appropriate pronominal form

Forms such as *wherein, wherewith*, etc., are called by Jespersen (*M.E.G.* § 10. 6) compound relative adverbs. These compounds must have been formed on the analogy of *herein, therewith* (in place of preposition + demonstrative pronoun—see § 40); they date from the beginning of the 13th C,[1] and are used principally where the antecedent is an inanimate or neuter substantive. Sweet's reason for the employment of these adverbs (*N.E.G.* I. 379), viz. "that lifeless objects are generally stationary, and hence often come to be looked at from a purely local point of view" is unsatisfactory, because the use is sometimes extended to personal antecedents, e.g. Malory, *Morte D'Arthur*, p. 711, 20 And it semed to Launcelot that above the preestes handes were thre men *whereof* the two putte the yongest by lykenes bitwene the preestes handes. See also example from *Volpone* below.

The use of compound relative adverbs reached its height in the 18th C, but has since the 19th C been regarded as formal and archaic, except in legal and official language.

E.M.I.H. I. 3. 145 (210) Send I these lines, *wherein* I do commence/ The happie state of true deserving lovers.

Sej. V. 170 (442) For, night hath many eies,/*Whereof*, though most doe sleepe, yet some are spies

Volp. I. 2. 56 (29) No, 'tis your Foole, *wherewith* I am so taken

Alch. II. 3. 183 (327) What else are all your termes,/*Whereon* no one o' your writers grees with other ?

---

[1] It should be noted, however, that *þǣr* (= where) . . . *on* occurs in O.E. with the force of a compound relative adverb, e.g., K. Alfred, *Greg. Past. Care* 51: Hēr is ān lytele burg, ðǣr ic mæg min feorh *on* generian.

49. How (= what) as interrogative

The original Germanic form of modern *how* was probably *hwó*. *Hū* was used in O.E. and M.E. (in the latter period also *hwu, hou* and in the 14th C *how*). Wyclif seems to have been the first writer to have used *how* in the sense of 'what' in direct questions. The *N.E.D.* gives more precise significations of the latter use as 'to what effect ?', 'with what meaning ?', 'by what name?'. *How* continued to be so employed until the first half of the 19th C.

But in indirect questions *how* (= what) was in use much earlier. An example occurs in Aelfric's *Homilies* (II. 310) þā āxode se cāsere þone ǣnne prēost *hū* his nama wǣre.

There is every indication that O.E. *hwā* (*hwæt*) and *hū* are from the same original stem, which may explain the early use of the latter for the former.

In exclamatory questions *how* for *what* also goes back to O.E. (see *N.E.D.* I. 4); this is now obsolete except in the colloquial phrase *how about* . . . ?

(*a*) *Direct questions*
  E.M.O.H. I. 2. 7 (444) for my name, Signior, *how* thinke you
  Revels I. 5. 6 (61) *how* art thou cal'd ?

(*b*) *Exclamatory questions*
  E.M.I.H. I. 1. 163 (201) *how* if thy Father should see this now

B. THAT

50. Early employment of 'that' as relative

The relative in O.E. took many forms (see S. O. Andrew, *Syntax and Style in O.E.*, ch. XII). The Teutonic languages were handicapped by their lack of a specific relative pronoun; and sooner or later most of them resorted to the demonstrative or interrogative pronouns, or to both. In English the demonstrative *sē, sēo, þæt* was first called into employment to take the place of *ðe*, mainly in descriptive clauses. *That* is, therefore, the oldest of the relative pronouns in modern use. Cf. the similar use of the demonstrative pronoun as a relative in the Greek of Homer.

Note: Jespersen (*M.E.G.* III, § 8. 7) prefers to regard *that* as a particle; Kruisinga (*English Studies*, Oct. 1924 and Feb. 1927) considers that it is a conjunction; both views are supported by a mass of evidence, which cannot be neglected. The retention of *that* as a relative pronoun is largely a matter of grammatical convenience, not of logical necessity.

C. BUT

51. Use of 'but' for relative in negative clauses

How the adversative conjunction *but* came to be used as a relative pronoun is not, so far as I can find, satisfactorily explained. Sweet (*N.E.G.* I. 417) says: "Adversatives add something which is unexpected, or at any rate, does not follow naturally from what has just been said." In the sentence 'No one remained *but* was sorry for it afterwards' *but* corresponds to Latin *quin*, and was probably an extension of the O.E. use of *būtan* in the Latin senses of *nisi*; so examples in Bosworth and Toller's *Anglo-Saxon Dictionary* would at least appear to indicate. *Būtan* was used in O.E. as adverb, preposition and conjunction; and these functions passed into M.E. and E.N.E.

The first use of *but* (= *who* (*that*) . . . *not*) recorded in the *N.E.D.* is at the beginning of the 16th century. At first the word was used only as a conjunction, being regularly followed by the personal pronoun, e.g. Jonson, *Discoveries*, ll 388-9 (575): There is almost no man, *but hee* sees clearlier and sharper, the vices in a speaker, then the vertues. This combination is often found at the present day.

By the middle of the 16th C there had appeared the parallel construction with the personal pronoun dropped, leaving *but* in the place of a relative pronoun. Both types were used only in negative clauses and questioning constructions. The usage is now obsolescent, but occurs frequently in poetry.

E.M.I.H. II. 2. 73 (224) what can I name,/*But* would become thee better then to beg ?

E.M.O.H. Induc. 363 (441) no honourable or reverend personage whatsoever, can come within the reach of his eye, *but* is turn'd into all manner of varietie

Revels I. 1. 10 (44) you ha' not a finger, *but* is as long as my quiver

D. DEFINING AND NON-DEFINING CLAUSES

52. The two types of clauses and their relative pronouns

A *defining* or *restrictive* relative clause is one which limits the antecedent, thereby making its meaning more precise. Without the necessary relative clause the antecedent would, in fact, be incomplete. The relative commonly used in modern English in such cases is *that*, and no comma separates it from its antecedent. It is used both for persons (as alternative to *who*, *whom*) and for things.

A *non-defining* or *non-restrictive* relative clause is one which leaves the meaning of the antecedent and the main clause unaffected. It supplies, as it were, a piece of gratuitous information. The relative commonly used in modern English is *which*, separated from the antecedent by a comma.

Note: *That*, when used as a relative, cannot be governed by a preceding preposition, whether the clause is defining or non-defining. The relative in such cases is *which*. *That* may, however, be used with preposition at the end of the sentence, e.g. These are the books *that* I came *for*. *Which* did not appear as a relative pronoun until the 12th C; *that* was thus used for both defining and non-defining clauses from the 9th—12th centuries. When *which* did appear as a relative pronoun, it was at first used only in non-defining clauses; but by the 14th C this precision had become blunted. In the 15th, 16th and 17th centuries *that* and *which* were used without much regard to their restrictive or non-restrictive function. The distinction is, indeed, too subtle for the man in the street, which accounts for the frequent disregard of it in modern colloquial speech.

(a) 'That' as general relative in non-defining clauses

This is comparatively common in Jonson.

E.M.I.H. III. 4. 123 (123) you lampe of virginitie, *that* take it in snuffe so

,, IV. 1. 43 (257) at one Cobs house, a waterbearers, *that* dwelles by the wall

,, IV. 3. 90 (265) a necessary question for you *that* are his wife

,, (F) I. 3. 61 (312) Hee cannot but thinke most vertuously, both of me, and the sender, sure; *that* make the carefull Costar'-monger of him

E.M.O.H. Char. 101 (426) An inseparable case of Coxcombs . . . Twins of foppery: *that* like a paire of woodden foyles are fit for nothing.

,, Ind. 134 (433) Good men . . . *that* lothe their vices,/ Will cherish my free labours

,, I. 2. 232 (451) 'tis an open-throated, black-mouth'd curre,/*That* bites at all

Revels I. 1. 23 (44) what are you ? any more then my uncle Ioves
pandar, a lacquey, *that* runnes on errands for him.
Alch. I. 3. 15 (309) I was wish'd to your worship, by a gentleman,/
One Captaine Face, *that* say's you know mens planets

(b) '*Which*' as general relative in defining clauses
This is much less frequent in Jonson than the uses of *that*
noted under (a).
Revels V. 11. 117 (179) 'Tis vertue *which* they want

E. EARLY N.E. EQUIVALENTS OF THE NEUTER RELATIVE 'WHAT'
OR 'THAT WHICH'

53. 'That . . . that' (demonstrative followed by relative), for modern 'that . . . which' (what)

Fowler in *The King's English* says : "If the antecedent happens
itself to be *that*, and the relative is to follow it closely, *that which*
must be used for *that that*, unless some substitute, as *what*, is
available." It is true that modern English, wherever possible,
avoids the conjunction (invariably defining) of demonstrative
and relative *that*, but it is used more frequently than is generally
supposed. It is quite regular after *It is*, the second *that* being
weakened to [ðət].

Jespersen (*M.E.G.* III, § 8. 33) thinks the modern reluctance
to use relative *that* in the circumstances noted is due to the
emphasis placed on the demonstrative, which weakens the
restrictive force of the succeeding *that*, and thus favours the use
of *wh-* relatives.

Historically, however, *that that* has had quite a long vogue.
It is found in O.E., is common in the *Ormulum* and indeed seems
to occur without intermission until the 17th century. Several
examples are found in Shakespeare and Jonson.

C.A. II. 3. 26-7 (129) It is Praecisianisme to alter *that*/With austere
iudgement, *that* is given by nature
E.M.I.H. II. 1. 6-7 (220) to have *that* outwardly in vilest estimation,
that inwardly is most deare
„ III. 1. 175 (237) Marrie *that*, *that* will make any man out of
love with them (F. *that which*. The alteration implies that *that*
that was probably falling into disfavour).
Poet. III. 4. 334 (256) but our Author will devise, *that*, *that* shall serve
in some sort.
Bart. F. III. 5. 252 (80) Would you ha' the boxe and all, Sir ? or onely
that, *that* is in't ?

Cf. Shakespeare *Henry VIII.* III. 2. 439 Mark but my fall and *that that* ruined me (Pope, editing, wrote *that which*)

   Note: Occasionally Jonson employs the modern *that which*:—
   E.M.O.H. V. 2. 40 (568) But *that which* transcends all, ladie; he doth so peerelessely imitate

54. Relative (or demonstrative) 'that' for 'that that', modern 'what' (that which)

The *N.E.D.* has pointed out the difficulty of determining whether *that* for *what* is a demonstrative or relative pronoun (see under *That*, demonstrative, B. 7, and *That*, relative, B. 3. a). The construction is probably elliptical, earlier combinations such as *that what* and *what that* being not uncommon; but it is by no means certain which part of speech has been omitted. Where it is emphatic, *that* is clearly a demonstrative, e.g. Shakespeare *Twelf. N.* V. 1. 153 Be *that* thou know'st thou art; Jonson, *Masque of Augurs* 319 (640) Who seeke for *that*, doth punish them to finde. But then most examples carry a mild degree of emphasis. Support for the demonstrative is found in the fact that this use of *that* can be preceded by a governing preposition, whereas relative *that* cannot, e.g.

Shakespeare, Sonnet 25. 4 Whilst I . . ./Unlooked for joy in *that* I honour most

Com. of Errors I. 1. 96 Gather the sequel by *that* went before.

The use of *that* for modern *what* is found as early as K. Alfred's translation of *Boethius* and as late as William Morris's translation of the *Odyssey*, though the latter is probably an archaism. The neuter relative *what* without antecedent is found as early as the 13th C, but did not come into regular use until the 17th C; it is extremely rare, for instance, in the *Authorized Version of the Bible*.

C.A. III. 2. 45 (142) I beseech your worship make no question/Of *that* you wish

E.M.I.H. II. 3. 139 (230) I lend no credit to *that* is reported of them

E.M.O.H. Induc. 335 (440) This is *that* our Poet calls Castalian liquor
   ,,   V. 7. 69 (587) can you aske me to pay *that* I never drank for

Sej. I. 103 (358) Tis true, *that* Cordus say's

Cat. I. 256 (443) Nay, urge not *that*/Is so uncertaine

Bart. F. III. 5. 244 (79) *That* you are to undertake, is this

D.A. I. 6. 154 (182) Troth, Sir, 'tis more then true, *that* you have uttred

Mag. La. III. 5. 70 (556) being an oppilation,/In *that* you call the neck o' the money bladder

Note: The difficulty of determining the part of speech is scarcely felt in the following:—

Epic. II. 4. 72 (189) Wilt thou ascribe *that* to merit, now, was meere fortune ?

Stap. N. V. 3. 26 (373) too much protestation/Makes *that* suspected oft, we would perswade.

Here *that* is clearly demonstrative, and the point of grammatical interest is the omission of the relative. But the constructions bear comparison with the examples listed above, the difference residing only in the position of *that*.

55. Relative 'which' for modern 'what' (that which)

This is related to the two preceding sections, and is thus for convenience included here. *Which* may be regarded as a condensed relative like *what*; or, as is more likely, the demonstrative antecedent *that* may be omitted.

E.M.I.H. V. 3. 327 (285) and *which* is most;/Crown'd with the rich traditions of a soule

Sej. III. 512 (409) The only gaine, and *which* I count most faire/Of all my fortunes, is that mightie Caesar/Hath thought me worthie his alliance

Epic. 2nd Prol. 15 (164) They make a libell, *which* he made a play (= They make *that* a libel, *which* he made a play).

Examples like the first, where the relative *which* is used with predications in the comparative or superlative degree, are common in Shakespeare e.g.

Mid. N. Dream, I. I. 103 And, *which* is more than all these boasts can be,/I am beloved of beauteous Hermia.

F. OMISSION OF RELATIVE

The relative is omitted in modern English mainly when it is a defining *that* and object of the verb in the relative clause.

56. Omission of nominative relative

A list of examples, mainly predicative, in which the nominative relative can be omitted in modern English is given in Curme aud Kurath's *Grammar of the English Language* (Vol. III, § 23 II. 10 a, page 235). A full treatment of the subject appears in Jespersen's *M.E.G.* III, § 7. 5₃ *et seqq.* The omission of the nominative relative can be traced to Middle English, numerous examples occurring in Chaucer; it survives in the modern English dialects (see Wright's *Dialect Grammar*, § 423). In N.E. the omission is often a stylistic mannerism peculiar to certain authors. Jonson and Shakespeare are particularly fond of it, especially in the following circumstances:

(*a*) *After here (there) is (are) etc.*
E.M.I.H. I. 1. 90 (199) here be them$_\Lambda$ can perceive it
   ,,   I. 3. 88 (209) ther's a gentleman below$_\Lambda$ would speake with you.

(*b*) *After He is, it is, that (this) is etc.*
T.T. 1. 5. 27 (20) Hee is the man$_\Lambda$ shall carry it
E.M.I.H. V. 3. 187 (281) twere pittie of his life$_\Lambda$ would not cherish such a spirite
Volp. I. 3. 2 (32) Onely you/(Of all the rest) are he,$_\Lambda$ commands his love

(*c*) *After interrogative pronoun + verb to be (Who is . . . etc.)*
E.M.I.H. III. 5. 2 (253) what cuckold is that$_\Lambda$ knockes so hard ?

(*d*) *After the common notional verbs have, see, think, know, etc.*
E.M.I.H. II. 3. 99 (228) I was thinking of a most honourable piece of service$_\Lambda$ was perform'd
   ,,   III. 5. 19 (254) I have it heare$_\Lambda$ will sause him
E.M.O.H. I. 2. 68 (446) I have a neece$_\Lambda$ is a marchants wife

(*e*) *Other omissions (sometimes metrical)*
Revels I. 2. 93 (51) Fond Eccho, thou profan'st the grace$_\Lambda$ is done thee (verse)
Sej. I. 357 (367) Why, this indeed is physick ! and out-speakes/ The knowledge of cheape drugs, or any use/$_\Lambda$ Can be made out of it !
Volp. I. 4. 70 (37) Here, I have brought a bag of bright cecchines,/$_\Lambda$ Will quite weigh downe his plate.
Cat. III. 192 (475) make on, upon the heads/Of men, strooke downe, like piles; to reach the lives/Of those$_\Lambda$ remaine, and stand
Bart. F. II. 2. 17 (41) I'll finde a friend$_\Lambda$ shall right me (prose)

Note (1) Elizabethan and Jacobean English was lax in the use of prepositions with the relative pronoun. Consequently omissions occur representing a potential relative in an oblique case, governed by the appropriate preposition:
e.g. E.M.O.H. I. 1. 17 (197) Fed with the self-same humor$_\Lambda$ he is now (= Mod. English 'with which')
(2) Comparable with the periphrastic constructions described in § 24 of the companion to this volume, *The Accidence of*

Ben Jonson's Plays, Masques and Entertainments are the following, in which relative *that* is omitted:

E.M.I.H. III. 4. 205 (253) One∧ they call *him* signior Lorenzo
E.M.O.H. Induc. 356 (441) He is one,∧ the author calls *him* Carlo Buffone.

G. CASE

57. Use of common relative with different case functions

Fowler, in his *M.E.U.* (*That*, relat. 5), writes: "It is quite in order to let a relative *which* or *that* carry on and serve a second clause as well, but only if three conditions are satisfied: the antecedent of the two must be the same; both must be defining, or both non-defining; and the case of the relative must be the same."

The second of these conditions is discussed under D; the third has always been of doubtful validity, seeing that the distinction between cases was lost before the modern period. But it would be wrong to assume that the custom is more honoured in the breach than in the observance. In fact, as examples below show, the modern ear is often offended.

Fowler requires that the relative *that* or *which* should be repeated in the second clause, if it fulfils a different case function. The omission in Jonson is generally attributable to poetic licence.

E.M.O.H. I. 1. 9-10 (442) Tis like a potion *that* a man should drinke,/ But∧ turns his stomache
Sej. II. 131 (379) I'le have an excellent new fucus made,/Resistive 'gainst the sunne, the raine, or wind,/*Which* you shall lay on with a breath, or oyle,/As you best like, and∧ last some fourteene houres (Here both *which* and *shall* are understood).

INDEFINITE RELATIVES

58. Use of whoso(ever), who, what, which, as indefinite relatives

In Shakespeare's "*who* steals my purse steals trash", the meaning of *who* is, 'whoever', 'anyone who', 'he who'. In N.E. *whoso*, *whosoever* are found performing the same function. These seem to be generalized or indefinite pronouns; they can hardly be regarded as relative pronouns, seeing that in their earlier history they required no antecedent. The name given to them in many grammars is 'indefinite relatives', though even this term is unsatisfactory (see Jespersen, *M.E.G.* III § 3. 1 *et seqq.*).

70

The common O.E. indefinite forms of the interrogatives *hwā*, *hwæt*, *hwilc* were *swā-hwā-swā*, *swā-hwæt-swā*, *swā-hwilc-swā*. In E.M.E. the initial *swā* was lost, and the second weakened, giving the forms *hwa . . . se* (*Ormulum*), *whattse* (*Ormulum*) and *hwuche . . . se* (*Ancren Riwle*). Unemphatic *se* soon tended to disappear, or to be replaced by *þat*. It remained, however, in the N.E. forms *whoso*, *whatso*, *whichso*.

Kellner gives, as an instance of *hwā* used as a relative pronoun, the following quotation from Wulfstan (ed. Napier, 95, 19): þæt dēofol openlīce þone fandige, *hwā* him fulfylligean wille. It is usually considered, however, that *who* as relative pronoun owes its existence to the earlier employment of *who* as an indefinite pronoun. In fact, the Wulfstan example contains a pronoun of this generalized type (modern *he who*), and translated would mean 'the devil tempts *him who* will follow him'.

The usual indefinite relatives in Shakespeare and Jonson are *who*, *whoso* (rare), *whosoever* (rare), *what*, *whatsoever* and *which*. *Who, whoso, whosoever* and *whatsoever* are now archaic except in traditional and proverbial expressions.

(*a*) *Who*

E.M.I.H. II. 2. 19 (223) Even so in man *who* searcheth soon shal find

Revels I. 2. 102 (51) And with thy water let this curse remaine, . . . that *who* but tastes/A drop thereof, may, with the instant touch,/Grow dotingly enamour'd on themselves

Poet. Prol. 7 (205) know, 'tis a dangerous age:/Wherein, *who* writes, had need present his Scenes/Fortie-fold proofe

Sej. I. 539 (373) And, *who* will search the reasons of their acts,/Must stand on equall bases

Cat. III. 143 (473) *Who's* angrie at a slander, makes it true

N. Inn III. 1. 62 (446) As *who* would say, take heed Sᶜrah (= as if one said)

Cf. Shakespeare, *Merch. of Ven.* I. 2. 42 He doth nothing but frown; as *who* would say, if you will not have me, choose. The construction dates from the late 13th C, and Jespersen suggests the influence of French *comme qui dirait*.

Note (1) *Who* also appears as indefinite relative in the plural (= those who)

Mag. La. Chor. I. 36 (528) Because, *who* expect what is impossible, or beyond nature, defraud themselves.

Note (2) The indefinite relative is occasionally found in oblique cases:

Revels V. 7. 9 (165) she . . . advised them wholy to consecrate themselves to thy celestiall service, as in *whose* cleere spirit . . . they should behold not her alone . . . but themselves . . . to live inthroniz'd (= someone in whose)

Epic. V. 4. 189 (269) I will become, *whose* slave you will give me to for-ever

(b) *Whoso*

Revels V. 4. 338 (149) *who so* strives to keep . . . he doth indeed smell farre worse

Cf. Shakespeare *Henry IV*, Part I, III. 4. 38 the law of arms is such/That *whoso* draws a sword

(c) *Whosoever*

C.A. II. 1. 55 (126) take out the key,/That *whosoever* peepes in at the key-hole,/May yet imagine there is none at home.

Hymenæi 720 (234) But *whosoe're* thou be, in this disguise,/Cleare Truth, anon, shall strip thee to the heart

(d) *What*

(i) *Adjectival uses*

E.M.O.H. I. 2. 150 (448) make you a Coat of armes, to fit you of *what* fashion you will

Sej. V. 304 (448) Better, my lord, withdraw,/You will betray *what* store, and strength of friends/Are now about you (a possible meaning here may be 'what degree of')

(ii) *Pronominal uses*

E.M.O.H. V. 5. 30 (580) ply 'hem with all manner of shot . . . or any thing *what* thou wilt

E.M.O.H. V. 6. 56 (584) turne it selfe into the shape of your dogge, or any thing (*what* you will). 'What you will' seems to have been an alliterative cliche, c.f. sub-title of Shakespeare's *Twelfth Night*.

D.A. III. 3. 224 (220) Leave you your doubting./And doe your portion, *what's* assigned you

e) *Whatsoever*

Volp. II. 6. 45 (63) and there, all your hopes, Venters, or *whatsoever*, are all frustrate.

Hymenæi 573 (229) Nor was there wanting *whatsoever* might give to the furniture

Cf. Shakespeare, *Hamlet* I. 2. 248 *whatsoever* else shall hap to-night

Note:—A nonce use of *whatsoever* with attributive indefinite function occurs in Jonson:

Revels V. 6. 61 (163) Not, for the empire of the universe,/Should night, or court, this *whatsoever* shine,/Or grace of ours unhappily enjoy. (The meaning is somewhat obscure, but *shine* appears to be used as a substantive)

(f) Which (of two)

Sej. IV. 412 (432) These letters make men doubtfull what t'expect,/ Whether his coming, or his death. *Pom.* Troth, both:/And *which* comes soonest, thanke the gods for

Epic. IV. 5. 32 (236) *which* of 'hem comes out first, will I seize on

Stap. N. Inter. IV. 71 (364) *Cen.* In two large sheetes of paper— *Exp.* Or to stand in a skin of parchment, (*which* the Court please)

N. Inn II. 1. 83 (426) *Pru.* . . . will you but please to aske him,/ Or let me make the motion ? *Lad. Which* thou wilt, Pru.

INDEFINITE

For the sake of convenience words used both pronominally and adjectivally are treated together. As a useful means of grouping, Jespersen's subdivisions of the Indefinite Pronouns (*vide* chs. XVII and XVIII of *The Essentials of English Grammar*) are preserved here.

I. INDEFINITE UNITY

59. (i) Use of 'one' with meaning of (a) somebody (b) anybody; (ii) adjectival use of 'one' meaning 'some'

(i) (*a*) Examples in the *N.E.D.* show that the use of *one* for 'somebody' dates from the late 13th C and that it survived until the 18th C. It is common in the plays of both Jonson and Shakespeare. The origin is almost certainly the O.E. numeral *ān* and not French *on* (from Latin *homo*), as has been suggested, though the French construction may have influenced its adoption. *An* simply took the place of the O.E. impersonal indefinite pronoun *man*. But the change over was gradual, the two words being used side by side until the 15th C. In Malory's *Morte d'Arthur*, where *man* is regularly used, *one* is substituted for it if the reference is to a feminine person.

E.M.I.H. III. 1. 109 (235) let *one* straight bring me word

„ IV. 1. 27 (257) I was going along . . . when (of a suddayne) *one* calles

E.M.O.H. II. 6. 100 (492) bring me a cloake there, *one*

Poet. V. 3. 130 (301) *One* fit him with a paire of larger eares:/ 'Tis Caesars doome

Sej. II. 481 (391) *One* met Eudemus, the Physician,/Sent for but now: who thinkes he cannot live.

Epic. IV. 2. 13 (223) Gentlemen, I have plac'd the drum and the trumpets, and *one* to give 'hem the signe when you are ready.

Alch. II. 5. 70 (336) they have heard, since/That *one*, at Heidelberg, made it, of an egge

(*b*) Jonson's unique use of *one* for 'anybody', quoted below, seems rare.

E.M.O.H. IV. 1. 17 (529) I have as much cause to bee melancholy, as *one* (= anyone)

(ii) The modern indefinite use of *some* in the expression '*some* place *or other*' is first found, according to the *N.E.D.*, in Shakespeare:

Com. of Errors I. 2. 95 By *some* devise *or other*,/The villaine is ore-wrought of all my monie.

If this construction is as late as the end of the 16th C, it was probably not a settled usage until the 17th C. *Another* is often found in place of *other*.

Jonson has the peculiar adjectival use of *one* in the place of *some*. I can find no similar example in the *N.E.D.*

Epic. III. 3. 86 (206) The smell of the venison, going through the street, will invite *one* noyse of fidlers, or other (here *noyse* = band)

II. PRONOUNS OF DIFFERENCE (OTHER, ANOTHER)

60. Use of (a) 'another' for modern 'someone (anyone) else' (b) 'no other' for 'nothing else'

(*a*) In O.E. *ōðer* (Gothic *anþar* = one of two) performed the functions of modern *another*. The latter did not appear until the 13th C, adjectival uses apparently being earlier than pronominal ones. *Another*, with the meaning 'someone else', is first quoted in the *N.E.D.* from *Ayenbyte of Inwyt* (1340). Its use in religious prose and poetry is not uncommon in the 18th and 19th centuries, but it is now archaic.

T.T. I. 1. 59 (13) Che can spy that/At's little a hole, as *another*, through a Milstone

E.M.I.H. IV. 2. 134 (262) *another* might have tane it up as well as I

E.M.O.H. IV. 7. 20 (553) I have as good a body in clothes, as *another*

74

Revels V. 2. 12 (132) I hope we shall find wit to performe the science as well as *another*

Note: (i) *Another* is infrequently used adjectivally with the meaning of 'a different'.

Mag. La. IV. 2. 38 (566) I cast mine eye long since,/Upo' the other wench . . ./*Another* manner of peice for handsomenesse,/Then is the Neice

Note: (ii) The original O.E. use of *other* is sometimes retained, either adjectivally or pronominally:—

Cat. III. 636 (489) Gabinius, you, with *other* force, shall stop/The pipes, and conduits (= another)

Alch. II. 3. 183 (327) What else are all your termes,/Whereon no one o' your writers grees with *other* (= another).

(*b*) *No other* for 'nothing else' occurs infrequently in both Jonson and Shakespeare. Similar combinations, with apparently the same meaning, are sometimes found in O.E. and M.E., e.g. *nouht ōpres* in K. Alfred's *Boethius* and *nanoper* in *Cursor Mundi*.

Epic. I. 3. 4 (173) *Cle.* . . . True-wit's a very honest fellow. *Daup.* I thinke *no other*: but this franke nature of his is not for secrets.

Cf. Shakespeare, *Macbeth* V. 4. 8. We learn *no other* but the confident tyrant/Keeps still in Dunsinane

61. 'Other' used adjectivally before numerals

This construction can be traced back to O.E. (see *N.E.D.* under *Other* A. 5. d.). *Other* is an adjective qualifying a numeral, where modern English would use it as a pronoun in the plural, qualified by the numeral, i.e. '*other* three' would be 'three *others*'. This adjectival use of *other* seems to have survived until the 18th century. 'Other three' is, in fact, still good Scots.

E.M.O.H. II. 6. 33 (490) I had *other* three

Masque of Beauty 74 (183) made report, how *other* foure/Of their blacke kind . . ./Had followed them

62. Pronominal use of 'else' as synonym for 'other'

O.E. *elles* was an adjective in the genitive case used adverbially, as in modern English. The genitive of substantives and adjectives was frequently so used. In the following example, rare in Jonson, *else* is elliptical for 'anyone else'; and this usage seems confined to the 16th C.

E.M.I.H. III. 1. 114 (236) Or whether he come or no, if any other,/
Stranger or *else* ? faile not to send me word
Cf. Shakespeare, *King John* II. 1. 276 Bastards, and *else.*

III. PRONOUNS OF INDIFFERENCE (ANY, ERE A, EITHER)

63. 'Any' for modern 'anybody (anyone)'

The N.E.D. describes O.E. *ænig* as an indeterminate derivative
of *ān*. Its pronominal use, with the modern meaning of 'anybody', occurs as early as the *Lindisfarne Gospels* (c 950):
Mark XI. 16. And ne gelēfde þætte *ænig* oferfērede fæt ðerh þām
tempel
Anybody and *anyone* both began to appear in the 15th C, but
were not in common use until much later; *any* continued to be
current until the 18th C, but is now only used absolutely in
the plural.

E.M.O.H. Induc. 140 (433) If *any*, here, chance to behold himselfe,/
Let him not dare to challenge me of wrong

64. Use of 'any' with appositional superlative

The construction is found in Jonson and Shakespeare after
one, e.g. *Gypsies Metamorphosed* 370 (577) Shee is sister of a
Starre,/*One the noblest* nowe that are; *Henry VIII*, II. 4. 48 My
father, king of Spain, was reckon'd *one*/*The wisest prince* that
there had reign'd by many/A year before. This may be an imitation of the Latin *fortissimus unus*. Chaucer uses this appositional
superlative more frequently than Shakespeare; but he also has
the alternative construction with the partitive genitive, as used
in modern English (*one of the wisest princes*). The construction
is not, however, confined to *one*. It is found in Jonson with the
indefinite pronoun *any*.

Revels V. 6. 57 (163) if . . ./We but discover'd . . ./*Any, the least* of
imputations stand/Readie to sprinkle our unspotted fame (The
possibility of *any* being an adverb must not be ruled out. The
phrase may mean 'even the least imputation'. Or an ellipsis of some
sort of adverbial modification may be postulated, e.g. '*any* imputation, *no matter how small*')
Sej. Readers 33 (351) their whole Bodies, like Moles, as blindly working
under Earth to cast *any, the least*, hilles upon Vertue.

65. Use of 'any' meaning 'any sort of'

This usage, though far from rare, does not appear in the
N.E.D. until the 19th C.

Cat. IV. 708 (520) *Semp*. When come these creatures, the Ambassadors?/ I would faine see 'hem. Are they *any* schollers ?/*Len*. I think not, madame.

Cf. a similar negative construction:

Epic. II. 3. 110 (186) Why ? every man that writes in verse, is not a Poet; you have of the Wits, that write verses, and yet are *no* Poets

66. Ellipsis of 'anything' before preposition 'but'

This common ellipsis, especially after negative constructions with the verb 'to be', is first cited in the *N.E.D.* from Lord Berner's translation of Froissart. It seems to have maintained its popularity at least as late as the 19th C.

E.M.O.H. II. 1. 179 (465) it cannot be$_\wedge$ *but* a most pleasing object.

67. Use of 'ever (ere) a' for 'any . . . at all'; 'never (nere) a' for 'no . . . at all'

These uses are almost certainly emphatic. The original combination seems to have been *ever any*. An example occurs in L.O.E. (see *N.E.D.* under *Ever*, II. 8. a):

c. 1067 Charter of Edward in *Cod. Dipl.* IV. 219, Ic nelle ðat *efre* ani bisscop ani þing him ðer on a ateo (where *efre* seems to be an emphatic adverb).

In E.M.E. weakening of O.E. *ǽnig* to *ǽi* or *ei* occurred (examples are numerous in Layamon's *Brut* and the *Ancren Riwle*); and this may have been the source of *ever(e're) a* which was the regular combination from the 16th—18th C. Similarly there arose the negative *never (ne're) a*.

These emphatic uses, as Wright has shown, are common in the English dialects. *Ever a* is now distinctly bucolic; but *never a* has remained in modern Standard English.

(*a*) E.M.I.H. I. 1. 29-30 (198) Can you tell me, and he have *e're a* booke of the sciences

     ,,   III. 4. 16 (247) they should have beene damn'd e're they should have come in, *e're a* one of them

Revels IV. 1. 43 (100) would I might never dare to looke in a mirror againe, if I respect *ere a* marmoset of 'hem all

Stap. N. Inter I. 64 (303) and lov'd the common wealth, as well as *e're a* Patriot of 'hem all.

(*b*) E.M.O.H. II. 3. 189 (475) There's *ne're a* one of these, but might be a weeke on the racke

Volp. V. 4. 49 (119) Ha' you *ne're a* curren-but to leape into ?

Stap. N. I. 3. 53 (292) Give me *never a* penny,/If I strike not thorow your bounty with the Rowells.

68. Use of 'either' for choice of more than two, where modern English requires 'any'

In O.E. *ǣʒhwǣðer, ǣʒðer* had the meaning 'each of two'; the *N.E.D.* says that about 1300 it began to take on the disjunctive meaning of 'one or the other of two', which persists to the present day. The use of *either* for a choice of more than two is frequent in the 16th C (the *N.E.D.* has no examples earlier than 1588). It is still in use, but is generally regarded as a solecism.

E.M.O.H. II. 2. 24 (466) To the perfection of complement . . . are required these three specials: the gnomon, the puntilio's, and the superficies . . . in *either* of which, for a stranger to erre, 'tis easie and facile

„   III. 1. 31 (497) reading the Greeke, Italian, and Spanish; when he understands not a word of *either*

IV. PRONOUNS OF UNSPECIFIED QUANTITY (SOME, SOMEWHAT, WHAT)

69. Adjectival (or adverbial) use of 'some' (= about a) with periods of time, quantities, etc.

In the expression '*some* six years ago' the function of *some* is very like that of an adverb of approximation; it modifies a numeral (or fraction). This usage goes back to O.E., e.g.

K. Alfred *Boethius* XXXVIII, 1. ðā hæfde hē *sume* hundred scipa (Bosworth and Toller, see under *sum* II. 4a, apparently regard *sume* as an adjective).

This employment of *some* is by no means obsolete, e.g. *some* hundred persons gathered in the hall.

E.M.I.H. I. 3. 112 (209) Faith *some* halfe houre to seven

70. Use of 'somewhat' and 'what' meaning 'something'

The M.E. indefinite pronoun compounded of *sum* (*som*) and *what* is first found in *The Ormulum* (beginning of 13th C), where it has the meaning of modern 'something'. It is still used in this way with a following genitive, e.g. It was *somewhat* of a surprise to me.

The use of *what* with the same or similar meaning is not so old; it occurs chiefly after the verbs *wot*, *know* and *tell*, and is common in idiomatic and colloquial expressions from Chaucer to the 19th C (see examples in *N.E.D.* under A. I. 8, where it is suggested that *what* in modern English 'Do you know *what* ?' and 'I'll tell you *what*' may be elliptical for '*what it is*'.)

(a) E.M.I.H. I. 1. 145 (201) hee may doe *somewhat* for his household
servants
 ,, I. 3. 39 (207) *somewhat* was in it
Sej. IV. 443 (433) It boded *somewhat*
Epic. V. 2. 67 (256) We lack him for *somewhat* else too
Alch. III. 1. 17 (341) Beside, we should give *somewhat* to mans
nature
Bart. F. I. 3. 30 (24) I agreed with Proctor Iohn heere, to come
and doe *somewhat* with Win
D.A. I. 4. 89 (175) I doe know *somewhat*, I forbid all lip-worke
N. Inn I. 3. 96 (413) Troth, I was borne to *somewhat*, Sir, above it

(b) Revels Epil. 6 (183) But if I yet know *what*, I am a rogue (verse—
what may be elliptical for *somewhat*)
 Cf. Shakespeare, *Richard III*, III. 2. 92 Wot you *what*, my lord ?/
To-day the lords you talk of are beheaded
Merch. of Ven. I. 1. 86 I tell thee *what* Anthonio, I love thee

V. PRONOUNS OF TOTALITY

A. *Positive* (all, both, every, each, etc.)

In modern English *all* expresses totality where more than
two are concerned, and *both* where only two are in question.
Every, which is only used adjectivally, (the pronoun proper
is *everyone*, with the partitive genitive) expresses separation;
the units of an unlimited group are considered individually.
Each, which is also a pronoun of separation, refers to the
units of at least a limited group, if not to two. These dis-
tinctions were not always clearly preserved in the 16th and
17th centuries.

71. Adjectival use of 'all' and 'both' before personal and wh-relative pronouns

(a) *All* (W.S. *eall*) was used absolutely in O.E.; the inflexions
show that it was an adjective used as a noun or pronoun.
All before a personal pronoun was common from L.O.E.
to the 17th C. *All* in the post-position is probably as early;
the *N.E.D.* has an example from the *Lambeth Homilies*
(c. 1175); and this is commonly used at the present day,
e.g. *we all*; *they all*. The alternative modern construction,
all used absolutely, followed by a substitute-partitive genitive, e.g. *all of us*, *all of them*, seems to date from the 16th C
only; the first example in the *N.E.D.* is from Shakespeare's
Richard II, III. 2. 142: Yea, *all of them* at Bristow lost
their heads.

All who and *all which* almost certainly date from E.N.E., but have become obsolescent in the modern period, giving place to *all* + substitute-partitive genitive, *all of whom*, *all of which*. The *N.E.D.* suggests that *all which* was not much used after 1850; but Jespersen (*M.E.G.* III § 6. 4₇) rightly points out that it can be used when the reference is to the whole of a preceding argument. *All what* is used by Shakespeare.

(i) C.A. II. 7. 136 (139) Say the Signe should be in Aries now; or it may be for *all us*

E.M.I.H. III. 418 (247) could I keepe out *all them* thinke you

Revels IV. 1. 3 (99) hee has left *all us* in travaile with expectation of it

Epic. II. 5. 55 (194) and doe you alone so much differ from *all them*

Bart. F. Induc. 92. 15 (483) And if he pay for halfe a dozen, hee may censure for *all them* too

(ii) E.M.O.H. II. 4. 86 (483) *all which*, now, I have alter'd

Sej. I. 172 (360) *All which* snares/When his wise cares prevented, a fine poyson/Was thought on

Epic. V. 3. 78 (259) twelve impediments (as we call 'hem) *all which* doe not dirimere contractum, but irritum reddere matrimonium

Cf. Shakespeare, *Timon* IV. 2. 35 To have his pomp and *all what* state compounds/But only painted.

(*b*) *Both* is from O.N. *báðar*; the forms found in O.E. are *bēgen* and *bā*. *Both* is found before personal pronouns from the 14th to 16th centuries, e.g. Caxton, *Jason* (37b): *Bothe they* toke a good palfraye.

Both which was still in use in the late 18th C (see example in Curme and Kurath *G.E.L.* III. 6 c, p. 30). Jonson has several instances, where *both of which* would now be used.

(iii) C.A. II. 5. 24 (133) Your lordship yet may trust *both* them with him

Cat. I. 207 (441) *Both* they . . ./ . . . gave me word, last night.

(iv) E.M.I.H. I. 1. 138 (201) Ile be so bold as reade it,/Be it but for the styles sake, and the phrase;/*Both which* (I doe presume) are excellent.

Revels V. 6. 89 (164) onely opportunitie doth want,/Not will, nor power: *both which* in him abound.

Alch. II. 3. 146 (326) It is, of the one part,/A humide exhalation, which we call/Materia liquida, or the unctuous water;/On th'other part, a certaine crasse, and viscous/Portion of earth; *both which*, concorporate,/Do make the elementarie matter of gold

72. 'All' meaning (a) 'every' (b) 'everything'

The first is an adjectival use, the second a pronominal (absolute) use, and both occur in O.E. (See *N.E.D.* under *all* A. I. 3 and II. 8.) When *all* in the adjectival function first appears with the meaning 'every', it is found only before *þing*, e.g.

c. 1000 Ælfric, *Saints* L. I. 136. God ælmihtiჳ wāt *ealle þing* tōgædere

The *N.E.D.* suggests that from such collocations, in which singular and plural were alike, *alle thing* came to be regarded as a collective and finally as a singular. This may account for the employment of *all* in the sense of 'every'. Except in idiomatic phrases like *all manner of* and *all kind of* this use did not survive the 17th C.

The absolute use of *all* for 'everything' still serves a very useful purpose. It is commonly employed predicatively, e.g. 'that is *all*', and in the phrase '*all in all*'.

(*a*) E.M.I.H. III. 4. 8 (247) *all* maner of villany
 Revels V. 6. 72 (163) But Phoebe lives from *all*, not onely fault,/But as from thought, so from suspicion free
 Cf. Shakespeare, *Macbeth* III. 1. 14 And *all* thing unbecoming

(*b*) E.M.O.H. I. 2. 45 (445) studie their carriage, and behaviour in *all*
 Volp. IV. 6. 80 (107) looke, that *all*,/What ever, be put in
 Love Freed from Ignorance 287 (368) The King's the eye, as we do call/The Sunne the eye of this great *all*. (Substantival use = the universe)
 Cf. Milton, *Par. Lost* I. 105 *All* is not lost

73. Use of 'all' + def. article + noun in plural, where modern English has def. article + only + noun in singular

In Jonson this is a nonce usage. I have been unable to trace a similar example in the *N.E.D.*

N. Inn. I. 3. 3 (410) He's *all* the sonnes I have Sir (= the only son)
Cf. Shakespeare, *Twelfth Night* II. 4. 123 I am *all* the daughters of my father's house.

74. Use of 'every' with appositional superlative (See parallel use of *any* under Pronouns of Indifference, § 64)

This idiomatic use of *every* (from O.E. *æfre ælc*) does not appear as early as the comparable uses of *one* and *any*; it is most commonly found in the expression *every the least*. The *N.E.D.*, which

has an example from the late 18th C, says that the use of *every*
+ *the* + a superlative adjective is now outmoded, the sense being
expressed by *even the least* etc., treated as a parenthesis. Jonson
has the construction with the familiar possessive pronoun *your*
in the medial position.

Revels II. 3. 17 (70) the particular, and distinct face of *every* your most
  noted species of person.

75. Distributive use of 'everyone' after personal pronouns

The modern preference is for the absolute use of *everyone*
followed by the substitute-partitive genitive, e.g. *everyone* of
you. Actually this is also the earliest way that *everichon* was
used, the first example in the *N.E.D.* being

c. 1225 *Ancren Riwle* 18. Blesciðð ou mid *everichon* of ðeos
gretunges

The alternative construction, noun or pronoun followed by
everyone, was commonly used alongside of this from the 13th C to
the end of the 17th C, when it began to give way to the original
order. The post position, infrequent in Jonson, is by no means
out of date today.

E.M.I.H. V. 1. 75 (272) Ile have *you everyone* before the Doctor

76. Use of 'each' meaning (a) every (b) each of all

(*a*) In its origin *every* (= ever each) was merely a compound
   of *each* (O.E. ǣlc). The early uses of *each* convey the sense
   of 'every' very frequently, e.g. O.E. Chronicle 1101 Rotb't
   ælce ʒeare sceolde . . . þreo þusend marc habban.

   In modern English *each* has become restricted mainly to
   distributive uses where only a few are in question; and
   every to uses where an unlimited number are in question.
   When this refinement of meaning came about is not certain,
   but it is unlikely that it took place before the 18th C. *Each*
   and *every* are used in similar ways by most 16th and 17th
   century writers up to and including Milton, e.g. Spenser
   F.Q. I. 2. 8 She *every* hill and dale, *each* wood and plaine did
   search. (See also examples quoted by Jespersen *M.E.G.*
   II. § 7. 812, last paragraph.)

   E.M.I.H. (F) I. 1. 70 (306) I would not have you to invade *each*
      place

   Cf. Milton, *Par. Lost* IX. 661 Of the fruit/Of *each* tree in the garden
      we may eat

(b) Dealing with the early use of *each* the *N.E.D.* says: "a
sentence with a singular subject preceded by *each* would
(formerly) have been but slightly if at all altered in meaning
by the substitution of a plural subject preceded by *all*"
(see under *Each* B. I. 1). The singular and separatist notion
of *each* was not in its earlier history clearly preserved.
Plural uses with the modern meaning of 'all' are quite common from L.O.E. to the end of the 16th C, and even in
modern English as grammatical solecisms.

In the following example from Jonson the idea of separate-
ness is, to some extent, retained.

> Cat. III. 718 (492) What ministers men must, for practice, use !/
> The rash, th'ambitious, needy, desperate,/Foolish, and
> wretched, ev'n the dregs of mankind,/To whores, and women !
> still, it must be so./*Each* have their proper place; and, in
> their roomes,/They are the best (= each of all these)
> *Cf.* Shakespeare, *Win. Tale* II. 3. 35 At *each* his needless heavings

77. Use of 'either' meaning (a) each one of two (b) both

(a) The 12th C word *eiðer* seems to be etymologically derived
from O.E. *ǣʒhwæðer* (ā + ge + hwæðer), the contracted
form of which was *ǣʒðer*. The original meaning was 'each
of two', which is still preserved in such expressions as 'on
either side of the river', condemned by most modern grammarians as ambiguous. It was not until the beginning of the
14th C that *either* acquired its modern meaning of 'one or the
other of two', which belonged to O.E. *āhwæðer*, M.E. *owþer*,
E.N.E. *outher*, still existing in English dialects and considered, wrongly, to be a bucolic form of *either*. As often
happened, the form of one word was thus represented by
the meaning of another, owing to similarity of sound and
spelling in M.E.

But the old meaning 'each of two' remained, was common
in the 16th and 17th centuries and did not become obsolete
until the 19th C. The combination *either ... other* was fairly
common from L.O.E. to the 19th C.

> C.A. IV. 2. 15 (150) I could have wisht some happier accident/
> Had made the way unto this mutuall knowledge,/Which *either*
> of us now must take of other
> E.M.I.H. (F) I. 1. 12 (304) a scholler ... in both our universities,/
> *Either* of which hath favour'd him with graces

Cf. Shakespeare, *Lucrece*, 66. Beauties red and Vertues white,/Of *eithers* colour was the other Queene.

Cf. also reciprocal use in Jonson's *Hymenæi* 756 (235) So men, or women are worth nothing neither,/If *eithers* eyes and hearts present not *either*.

(b) *Either* for 'both' is cited only three times in the *N.E.D.*, the last dated 1608. Both examples from Jonson are later than this. In the second example *his either* represents modern English 'both his'.

Cat. V. 501 (543) I see your faces, and your eyes/All bent on me, to note of these two censures,/Which I incline to. *Either* of them are grave

S.S. II. 7. 8 (39) his knees are lead;/And he can stirre his *either* hand, no more/Then a dead stumpe

Cf. Herrick, *Another Grace for a Child*, Here a little child I stand,/ Heaving up my *either* hand.

B. *Negative* (none, neither)

78. Idiomatic use of 'none' before 'such'

Nān was regularly used adjectivally in O.E.; it was the negative of *ān*. The reduced form *na* did not appear until the beginning of the 13th C, when it came into use before consonants, *nan*, *non* being then reserved for employment before vowels and *h*, in the same way as *an*, *mine*, *thine*. By the beginning of the 17th C, however, the adjectival use of *none* was rare, *no* having taken its place generally. *None* then continued in use only as a pronoun. In the combination *none such*, popular as late as the 19th C, *none* is probably a pronoun and *such* adjectival. The modern equivalent is 'nothing of that sort'.

E.M.I.H. V. I. 11 (270) I saw *none* such
Cf. Shakespeare, *Othello* IV. 2. 124 I am sure I am *none* such

79. 'None' meaning (a) nobody (b) no persons (c) not one

(a) *Nān* was used as a pronoun with the meaning 'nobody' in O.E. The N.E. form *none*, with this signification, began to fall into disuse in the 17th C; and although so used by Swinburne in prose in the 19th C, it is generally regarded as archaic, except in poetry.

C.A. II. 1. 56 (126) take out the key,/That whosoever peepes in at the key-hole,/May yet imagine there is *none* at home.

Revels IV. 5. 53 (127) *Hed.* . . . held the most accomplisht societie of gallants ! *Mer.* By your selves, *none* else.

Sej. II. 484 (391) Thinkes ? if't be arriv'd at that, he knowes,/ Or *none* (= or no one does)

Alch. V. 2. 7 (390) I left/*None* else, but thee, i' the house !

(*b*) The use of *none* for 'no persons' is merely the absolute use of the preceding in the plural, and is also found in O.E. The *N.E.D.* says that this is commoner than the singular, which is now expressed by *no one*. The example from *Cynthia's Revels* quoted above may, of course, be a plural use.

T.T. II. 3. 1. (33) here are *none*/But one friend (as they zay) desires to speake/A word, or two, cold with you

Note: *None* sometimes denotes 'not one' or 'no persons' of a group understood; in other instances it signifies complete nonentity. The modern English equivalent is 'nothing'.

N. Inn. Charac. 29 (403) iealous that her Lord lov'd her not, because she brought him *none* but daughters (= no children; modern English 'nothing').

Golden Age Restored 96 (423) Die all, that can remaine of you, but stone,/And that be seene a while, and then be *none* (= nothing at all)

(*c*) The predicative use of *none* meaning 'not one' (according to the *N.E.D.* 'denoting lack of the essential qualities of the thing or person mentioned') is found from O.E. to the 17th C, and is fairly common in both Jonson and Shakespeare. It is clearly emphatic.

E.M.I.H. II. 3. 174 (231) You said it was a Toledo ha ? . . . But it is *none*.

„ II. 3. 193 (231) I am *none* of that coate

Epic. I. 3. 29 (173) Hee is one of the Braveries, though he be *none* o' the Wits

Note: Emphatic *none*, followed by the prepositions *of*, *on*, in a partitive sense, as in the last two examples, is commonly found in the 16th and 17th centuries. But similar uses occur in which the sense is not partitive, as in modern English 'It was *none* of my business'. This is fairly common in Jonson and his contemporaries, and seems to carry the modern meaning of 'not at all', 'nothing at all', or 'not in any way'.

E.M.O.H. V. 3. 25 (572) I saw *none* of his dog, sir

Epic. IV. 1. 16 (219) it was *none* of his plot

80. The compound indefinite 'neither nother'

The nonce use of *neither nother* by Hilts in *A Tale of a Tub* is intended as a dialect form (presumably Yorkshire). The *N.E.D.* has two examples, one adjectival from Chaucer's translation of *Boethius*, and the other pronominal from *Political Poems* (Rolls Series) II. 95, dated 1401: As I wene the Holigost appreveth *nether nouther*. The double negative is probably emphatic. Jonson's use is pronominal.

T.T. II. 4. 41 (36) Tut, keepe your land, and your gold too Sir: I/Seeke *neither-nother* of 'hun.

RECIPROCAL

81. Word order in the reciprocal combinations 'each other', 'one another'

The so-called reciprocal pronouns of modern English, *each other* and *one another* are really indefinites. In modern English it is permissible to regard these as 'compound plural indefinites'; but originally, as Morris points out (*Historical Outlines of English Accidence* § 261), *each* and *one* were the subjects, and *other* and *another* the objects, of the actions described. Thus

Help each other = each help (the) other
Help one another = one help another[1]

The main interest lies in the position of the verb or preposition in relation to these combinations.

(a) *Each other*, which is the earlier combination historically, appears both as a distance-combination (components separated by verb or preposition) and as a juxtaposed combination, in the same work, in the 9th C. Examples are taken from the *N.E.D.*

K. Alfred, *Oros* I. 1. § 23 swā ǣlc æfter ōðrum
„   „   „ II. 3. § 2 Heora þǣr ǣʒðer ōðerne ofslōg

The former construction was commonly used as late as the 17th C; and, as an archaism, was still found in the 19th C,

e.g. Keats, *Isabel*, xxi. Each unconfines/His bitter thoughts to *other*.

[1] As Jespersen shows (*M.E.G.* II. § 7. 751 *et seqq.*) the notion that *each other* refers to two, and *one another* to more than two, has never been strictly observed, in spite of the fact that some grammars elevate it to a rule.

Tennyson, *Coming of Arthur* 7, many a petty king . . ./Ruled in this isle, and ever waging wars/*Each* upon *other*, wasted all the land.

Jonson occasionally preserves the separate grammatical function of the components in the same way. It seems that in the 16th and 17th C the separation is most usual when the pronoun is the object of a preposition.

E.M.I.H. I. 4. 213 (219) Still *each* of *other* catching the infection
Hymenæi 514 (227) And soft embraces bind,/To *each*, the *others* mind
Cf. Shakespeare, *Coriol.* (F₁) V. 6. 100 Pages blush'd at him, and men of heart look'd wond'ring *each* at *others*.

(*b*) *One another* does not appear juxtaposed until the first quarter of the 16th C: 1525 Tyndale's *Bible*, Galatians VI. 4. Beare ye *one anothers* burthen.

But the original combination *one the other* appears almost two hundred years earlier, and was not uncommon until the end of the 16th C.

1340 *Ayenbyte of Inwywt*, 115 ne harmi mid wrong *on þe oþer*
1597 J. King, *On Jonas*, We should spare *one the others* life

Separated grammatical function is found at least as early as L.M.E. and as late as the first quarter of the 17th C:

c. 1400 Mandeville, *Travels*, ch. XXIII, 16, þei maken signes *on* to *anoþer* as monkes don
1617 Moryson, *Itinerary*, II. 107 Neither . . . can we . . . often heare *one* from *another*

So Jonson:

Revels I. 1. 29 (45) sets the cushions in order againe, which they threw *one* at *anothers* head overnight

Jonson has an unusually late use of the distance-combination with intermediate verb:

N. Inn I. 3. 136 (414) iustling in,/And out still, as they *one* drove hence *another*:
Cf. Shakespeare, *Troilus* III. 3. 84 Do *one* pluck down *another* and together/Die in the fall.

4 . THE DEFINITE ARTICLE

An exhaustive treatment of the history and semantic development of the articles is to be found in P. Christophersen's dissertation *The Articles, A Study of their Theory and Use in English.* "An article", he says, "can only be used provided the thing meant is already foremost in the hearer's mind" (§ 36).

The definite article *the* began as a demonstrative pronoun, the form of which in O.E. was *se, sēo, þæt.*

82. Use of 'the' before names of languages, academic subjects, arts, etc.

This was very common from the 14th to the 18th century, and, according to the *N.E.D.*, survives in dialect.

E.M.I.H. (F) I. 1. 43 (305) more studied then *the* Greeke, or *the* Latin
E.M.O.H. III. 1. 30 (497) reading *the* Greeke, Italian, and Spanish
  ,,   III. 4. 28 (503) according to *the* Metaphisicks
Epic. II. 2. 121 (182) and then skip to *the* Mathematiques (so Alch. IV.
    1. 83 (362), N. Inn. II. 5. 18 (431) and Mag. La. II. 4. 14 (535)).
Stap. N. IV. 4. 91 (359) You, Cousin Fitton,/Shall (as a Courtier) read
  the politicks

83. Use of 'the' before titles of books, plays, poems, musical compositions, etc.

The first example cited in the *N.E.D.* is from *Ancren Riwle* (c. 1225). It became comparatively common in the 16th and 17th centuries, especially before works of literary art with a well-established reputation. It survives in modern English mainly before the better known works of classical antiquity, e.g. the Iliad, the Phaedo, the Satyricon, etc.

E.M.O.H. II. 3. 226 (477) as choise figures ... as any be i' *the Arcadia*

84. Use of 'the' before the appellation of the Deity

The use of the definite article to indicate uniqueness is not uncommon in modern English, e.g. *the* Messiah, *the* Saviour. But in the case of the modern exclamation 'Oh, Lord', the definite article is now omitted. There is a nonce example in Jonson of the definite article inserted.

E.M.I.H. (F) II. 3. 43 (329) Oh, *the* lord !

85. Use of 'the' before 'heaven' or 'heavens'

The definite article occurs before the singular and the plural[1] in both Jonson and Shakespeare, and is probably due to the influence of the Bible. The *Authorized Version of the Bible* uses the definite article rarely before the singular and regularly before the plural. Examples of the former (now obsolete) use are to be found in *Deuteronomy* XXVIII, 12, and XXXIII, 26; cf. also Shakespeare, *Two Gentlemen* IV. 2. 41 *The heaven* such grace did lend her. Only in such phrases as *the heaven of heavens* is *the* omitted before the plural in the Bible.

In the late 16th and early 17th centuries *the* before the singular is employed both in verse and prose. Metre or rhythm does not always appear to be a governing factor; the usage is left to choice. Before the plural, however, the definite article is regular and examples are not noted; (see *Neptune's Triumph* 335 (692), *Fortunate Isles* 474 (723), *Love's Triumph through Callipolis* 150 (740)).

E.M.O.H. II. 3. 49 (453) We must be patient, and attend *the heavens* pleasure. (Possibly a plural use.)

Masque of Augurs 429 (645) Here *the heaven* opened, and Jove, with the Senate of the Gods, were discovered (prose; so Chloridia 250 (758).)

86. 'The' before proper names of persons or places preceded by an adjective

A special use before names of persons in the vocative case is found in O.E., e.g.

Beowulf 1474 Geþenc nū, *se* mæra maga Healfdenes (quoted by Franz *S.G.* § 261).

The definite article before proper names preceded by an adjective began to be omitted in the 13th C, and by the late 16th and early 17th centuries was used sparingly (see statistics collected by Kellner, *H.O.E.S.*, § 219). It is still so used, especially if the person or place is distinguished or familiar, e.g.

Francis Thompson, *To Eng. Martyrs* 163 That utterance . . ./Of *the doomed* Leonidas.

E.M.I.H. V. 1. 10 (270) is not *the* young Lorenzo here?

E.M.O.H. Induc. 164 (434) Then *the* new London, Rome or Nineveh

,, I. 2. 238 (451) another minion/Of *the* old lady Chance's

---

[1] *The N.E.D.* notes that the Hebrew plural *shāmayim* was used in the Bible in the same sense as the singular, and this may account for the identity of meaning of *the heaven* and *the heavens* in Elizabethan and Jacobean literature.

87. Generic use of 'the'

The use of the definite article to indicate unique type, quality or function is very old, and examples in the *N.E.D.* (see under *The* B. II. 19-23) show that it frequently goes back to O.E. or M.E.

There are many sub-divisions of the generic uses. The following arrangement is convenient for examples found in Jonson:—

(*a*) *To denote the type of a class*
   E.M.I.H. (F) II. 4. 5 (331) as ominous a fruit, as *the* Fico

(*b*) *To mark the outstanding nature of a person or thing* (*often also emphatic*)
   E.M.O.H. II. 3. 204 (476) shee is *the* lady of a most exalted, and ingenious spirit
   Revels II. 4. 22 (77) she was thought to be *the* Dame-Dido, and Hellen of the court

(*c*) *To indicate that a person sustains the character intended*
   This is extremely common after the verbs *be*, *play* and *act*.
   Cf. modern English 'play the fool'.

   E.M.I.H. V. 3. 405 (287) do not you play *the* woman with me?
   Volp. Ded. 22 (17) they will easily conclude to themselves, the impossibility of any mans being *the* good Poet, without first being a good man.
   Bart. F. IV. 2. 40 (90) I cannot perswade my selfe, but he goes to grammer-schole yet; and plays *the* trewant, to day.

88. Use of 'the' instead of possessive pronoun with parts of the body

The earliest example in the *N.E.D.* of the use of the definite article instead of the possessive pronoun before nouns designating parts of the body is from earliest M.E. (1154—*O.E. Chronicle*). *The* may, of course, only be substituted for the possessive, if the person intended has been previously named. In M.E. and E.N.E. this usage was very common. By the 17th C, however, the possessive pronoun was used with about equal frequency. In modern English the possessive is regular, except after prepositions, e.g. She has become fuller *in the* face.

E.M.O.H. I. 2. 235 (451) A slave, that to your face will (serpent-like)/ Creepe on the ground . . ./And to your backe will turne *the* taile, and sting/More deadly then a scorpion

Revels I. 2. 27 (49) Th'untimely fate of that too beauteous boy,/ . . ./
  Who (now transformed into this drouping flowre)/Hangs *the* re-
  pentant head, back from the streame
Cf. Shakespeare, *Troil. and Cres.* III. I. 152 he hangs *the* lip at something.

89. 'The while' and 'the whilst'

In O.E. *hwīl* was a strong feminine noun. The accusative
(duration of time) preceded by the def. article was used as an
adverbial phrase, *þā hwīle* (M.E. *the while*), from about the 10th
C. The conjunctival phrase *þā hwīle þe* (*þæt*) was employed
earlier by Alfred the Great (see examples in *N.E.D.* under *While*
sb. I. 2. a). The later use of *while* as a conjunction is probably
an abbreviation of the latter phrase.

Whiles, which appeared in the 13th C, was formed by analogy
with the masculine genitives of nouns employed as adverbs; but
it occurs first as a conjunction, in a *Bestiary* (c. 1220). *Cursor
Mundi* has *þe quils*, used as an adverb. In the same work we
find the conjunctival use of *þe quylest*, final -*t* being intrusive,
as in *amongst* and *amidst*.

The use in M.E. and E.N.E. of *the while*(*s*) (as adv. phrase, or
conjunctive adverb) and *the whilst* (as conjunctival phrase) was
quite common; but, with the exception of the adverbial use of
the while, which persisted in literary English until the 19th C, the
combinations were probably archaic and poetical by the 17th C,
if not earlier.

In Jonson the forms with preceding definite article are used
mainly for the sake of metre.

(*a*) Mag. La. II. 2. 47 (531) Why is your Mistris sicke ?/Shee had her
  health, *the while* shee was with me.
(*b*) Sej. V. 777 (466) The fornace, and the bellowes shall to worke,/
  The great Seianus crack, and piece, by piece,/Drop i' the founders
  pit . . ./*The whilst*, the Senate . . ./Make haste to meet againe,
  and thronging cry,/Let us condemne him (conjunctive-adverbial
  phrase)
  Alch. III. 2. 76 (344) Nor shall you need, ore-night to eate huge
  meales,/To celebrate your next daies fast the better:/*The whilst*
  the Brethren, and the Sisters, humbled,/Abate the stiffenesse of
  the flesh.
So Hymenæi 342 (222).

90. Use of 'the' before 'many' and 'most'

(*a*) In the early 16th C *the* + the absolute adjective *many*
  began to be used in the sense of the Greek ὁι πολλοι, mean-

ing 'the great majority of people' or 'the common herd'. Examples in the *N.E.D.* show that it was used in prose by Burke, Coleridge and Matthew Arnold, so that it was certainly kept in literary use as late as the latter half of the 19th C. In prose it is now obsolescent, but survives in poetry.

> Alch. Reader 15 (291) Nay, they are esteem'd the more learned, and sufficient for this, by *the Many*, through their excellent vice of iudgement.

(*b*) The absolute use of the superlative *most*, as now used, seems to date from the 15th C. Towards the close of the 16th C Udall used a preceding definite article, and from then both constructions have been equally common, with the meaning of 'the majority of people'. Arnold used it in verse and Stevenson in prose in the 19th C. The regular usage today is without preceding *the*.

> Mag. La. Induc. 89 (510) *The most* of those your people call authors, never dreamt of any Decorum

91. Use of 'the' (a) before a gerund (b) between a preposition and a gerund (c) between 'worth' and a gerund

This subject is closely related to the historical development and function of the gerund. It is treated here as a matter of convenience.

In modern English (*a*) has the definite article only when the gerund is followed by a substitute genitive, e.g. *the giving of presents* is unwise; (*b*) retains *the* rarely and in idiomatic usage only, e.g. He could have had it for *the* asking; and (*c*) dispenses with the definite article altogether.

It is possible that the use of the definite article, first found in M.E., was originally designed to emphasize the substantival character of the form in *-ing*, and to differentiate it from the participle. Full appreciation of the grammatical function of gerund and participle does not appear to have been reached until the late 17th or early 18th C; hence the variety of constructions, with and without the preceding definite article.

(*a*) In M.E. *the* before a gerund, followed by a substitute genitive, appears to have been regular.

Mandeville, *Travels* ch. XXVI 31 *the* bowynge of the hed at þat
    hour betokened this (gerund as subject)
,,   *Travels* ch. XXI 32 the yle where he had herd . . . *the*
    callynge of oxen at the plowgh (gerund as object)

The use of the definite article was retained until the 17th
C, and is found occasionally in Jonson, who has a direct
object after the gerund as well as a substitute genitive.

(i) Alch. II. 3. 300 (331) *The* naming this Commander, doth con-
    firme it
    Bart. F. I. 6. 54 (37) *the* very calling it a Bartholomew-pigge, and
    to eat it so, is a piece of Idolatry
    Cf. Shakespeare, *Merch. of V.* I. 2. 109 you need not fear *the*
    having of any of these lords.
    Meredith, *Diana of the Crossways*, ch. XXXV *the* trusting
    a secret to a woman (this is exceptional in modern English)

(ii) Alch. IV. 3. 104 (371) *The* quickly doing of it is the grace

(*b*) In E.N.E. *the* was retained between a preposition and a
gerund, e.g.

Malory, *Morte D'Arthur* 298. 10 in *the* fallyng he brake his thigh
,,   ,,   439. 34 I thanke you moche for *the* tellyng
    of your name

The construction is found in Elizabethan and Jacobean
literature, (i) with direct object, (ii) with the substitute
genitive succeeding, and (iii) in the passive voice.[1]

(i) The direct object after the gerund is now only used in
    poetry. It is mainly so employed also by Jonson.

    Revels I. 4. 40 (65) I may doe wrong to your sufficiencies in *the*
    reporting them (prose)
    Poet. V. 3. 169 (302) till both the time and wee/Be fitted . . ./
    For *the* receiving so divine a worke
    D.A. IV. 2. 38 (232) I meant to have offer'd it/Your Lady-ship,
    on *the* perfecting the pattent
    Stap. N. I. 5. 44 (295) why should not they ha' their pleasure,/
    In *the* believing Lyes, are made for them

---

[1] About the beginning of the 16th C the gerund, like the infinitive, began
to dispense with the preceding definite article, and to take an object like any
finite verb, instead of the substitute genitive. Thus
    He praised him for *the* serving *of* his king
began to appear as the modern
    He praised him for serving his king.
The modern construction appears quite frequently in Shakespeare, e.g.
Jul. Caes. IV. 3. 3 For taking bribes.

N. Inn. II. 6. 156 (440) command,/Her Ladiship, pain of our high displeasure/and *the* committing an extreame contempt (The preposition *of* is here understood before the definite article)

Mag. La. II. 5. 37 (537) *Lad.* What will you move him to ?/ *Pol. The* making you a Countesse. (The preposition *to* is here understood.)

Cf. Shakespeare, *Alls Well* IV. 3. 3 On *the* reading it he changed almost into another man.

(ii) The use of the substitute genitive after the gerund is now archaic. Jonson employs it seldom, but Shakespeare uses it with comparative frequency.

Volp. II. 2. 231 (57) So short is this pilgrimage of man . . . to *the* expressing of it. (prose)

Cf. Shakespeare, *Hamlet III.* 3. 85 To take him in *the* purging of his soul,

Note: Jonson has a prose usage of both the substitute genitive and the direct object in close proximity.

Mag. La. Chor. I. 47-8 bathe their braines in laughter, to *the* fomenting *of Stupiditie* it selfe, and *the* awaking *any velvet Lethargy* in the House.

(iii) The use of the gerund in the passive is rare in Jonson.

Stap. N. Inter II. 60 (325) and such I feare it is, by *the* being barrell'd up so long.

(*c*) The use of *worth* (O.E. *weorð*, M.E. *wurð*) followed by a verbal noun is very old. In O.E. the word was followed by the dative infinitive, e.g.

Lindisfarne Gospels (Skeat) Luke 3. 16 Ne am ic wyrðe tō unbindanne ðuongas sceóea

In M.E., the infinitive (later uninflected) was also used, and this construction was still occasionally found in the 16th C, e.g.

1559 Clough in Burgon, *Life of Gresham* I. 225 It was sure a sight worth *to go* 100 myles to see it !

But a little earlier than this the construction *worth* + def. article + gerund began to be used, e.g.

1540 Palsgrave, *Acolastus* IV. 7. X (ii) b My corne . . . was not worth *the* cuttyng downe

This usage continued, mainly in verse, but sometimes in prose, until the early 19th C.

94

From examples in the *N.E.D.* it seems that the definite article before the gerund was first omitted (the modern construction) by Spenser. The two constructions existed side by side until the 18th C, when the former (with definite article) fell into disuse.

Jonson uses the definite article rarely.

> Bart. F. I. 1. 1. (19) A pretty conceit, and worth *the* finding (prose)

92. Use and omission of 'the' before (a) periods of time and (b) measurements (including numerals)

(*a*) (i) The definite article has, from the beginning of the N.E. period (1450), been commonly used before words denoting time, periods of time or seasons. The use seems in O.E. and M.E. to have been confined to the phrase *ða hwīle* (M.E. *þe while*). Some of these usages have been preserved in modern English; others have been lost. Only the latter, still found in Jonson, are recorded here.

> Poet. I. 2. 173 (214) Sir, Agrippa desires you to forbeare till *the* next week (prose)
> D.A. I. 6. 21 (178) Which of your great houses,/ . . ./ . . . send not forth/Something, within *the* seven yeere, may be laught at ?/I doe not say seven moneths . . ./ . . . but seven yeere, wife. (Clearly metrical, since in line 23 the def. article is omitted.)

(ii) There are a few instances of the omission of 'the' where it would be used in modern English. In the first example below the omission would, of course, be regular, if an adjective preceded, e.g. 'on *fine* afternoons'.

> Revels III. 1. 56 (83) to read them asleep in_Λ afternoones upon some pretty pamphlet (prose)
> Sej. IV. 468 (434) In_Λ mean time,/By his employments, makes him odious/Unto the staggering rout (verse)

(*b*) The use of *the* before measurements (usually preceded by a numeral) is rare in English, and is invariably dictated by metre.

> Volp. I. 5. 14 (41) Tell him, it doubles *the* twelfe caract (verse—the reference is to a pearl)

93. Use and omission of 'the' before abstract nouns

The employment of the definite article before abstract nouns has always been a matter of some uncertainty. Its use was fairly common in O.E., e.g.

Gregory, *Pastoral Care* III. 35 On ðǽre ʒesundfulnesse mon forgiett his selfes

As regards Elizabethan language Schmidt (*Shakespeare Lexicon*, p. 1201) holds the view that *the* is found "Before abstract terms seemingly used in a general sense, but in fact restricted by their particular application: torches are made to light . . . fresh beauty for the use, Ven. 164 (Venus has a certain use in mind)". Often the employment of *the* is metrical; but many cases cannot be explained in this way.

In modern English, where usage is more stabilized, the definite article is often required, more often dispensed with. Only the instances where *the* appears to be contrary to modern English usage are recorded below.

(*a*) *Use*

E.M.I.H. (F) I. 2. 130 (310) There is a way of winning, more by love,/And urging of *the* modestie, then feare

  ,,   (F) II. 4. 4 (331) my present profession looses *the* grace: and yet *the* lye to a man of my coat, is as ominous a fruit, as the Fico (prose)

  ,,   (F) II. 5. 25 (334) this in *the* infancie; the dayes/Of the long coate

E.M.O.H. IV. 8. 167 (562) therein his art appears most full of lustre, and approcheth neerest *the* life

Cat. III. 631 (489) I would have you, Longinus, and Statilius,/To take *the* charge o' the firing

(*b*) *Omission*

E.M.I.H. III. 4. 163 (252) My wife and sister they are˄ cause of this (metrical)

Revels I. 1. 32 (45) take˄ state of a President upon you at wrestlings (prose)

Note 1. Use and omission of the definite article after the preposition *at* calls for special consideration. It is found largely before superlative adjectives. In the late 13th, and in the 14th centuries, *the* is found in regular use in such phrases as *at the length, at the end, at the least, at the first, at the best, at the last*, etc. e.g.

c. 1300 *K. Alis*, 1668, Now *at the* erst, the messangers/Buth y-come.

But *at þe* appeared frequently in the coalesced form *atte*, e.g.

1297 *Rob. of Gloucester* 155 *Atte* laste þis Saxones by gonne forto fle
c. 1386 Chaucer, *Prol.* 125 after the scole of Stratford *atte* bowe

At the beginning of the 16th C *at length* etc. (without *the*) began to appear, and it has been suggested that this was a normal N.E. shortening of *atte* to *at*. The two usages are readily adaptable to metrical exigencies.

(i) *Use of 'the'*
    C.A. IV. 2. 60 (151) I thought you'ld dwell so long in Cypres Ile,/ Yould worship Maddam Venus at *the* length
    E.M.I.H. I. 3. 58 (208) you should have some now, would take him to be a gentleman at *the* least (prose)
    N. Inn IV. 3. 54 (467) We all look'd for a Lady,/A Dutchesse, or a Countesse at *the* least.
    E.M.I.H. I. 3. 224 (213) ile teach you that tricke, you shall kill him with it at *the* first if you please (Idiomatic = at once, immediately—prose)
    E.M.O.H. I. 2. 100 (447) you must keep your men gallant at *the* first (prose)

(ii) *Omission of 'the'*
    E.M.O.H. V. 2. 122 (571) she saw the gentleman as bright, as at noonday, she: shee decipher'd him at₍ₐ₎ first (= at once— prose)
    Alch. I. 4. 7 (313) Coming along, at₍ₐ₎ far end of the lane,/Slow of his feet, but earnest of his tongue
    Mag. La. III. 6. 19 (557) But if my Lord should heare I stood at₍ₐ₎ end/Of any quarrell, twere an end of me
    S.S. I. 5. 20 (18) a sharpe Iustice:/Or stay, a better ! when the yeare's at₍ₐ₎ hottest

Note 2. By analogy *the* was omitted after other prepositions, especially before superlative adjectives.

    Sej. I. 140 (359) For both were of₍ₐ₎ best feature, of high race,/ Yeer'd but to thirtie (metre)

94. Instrumental 'the': use and omission

(*a*) The instrumental case of the O.E. demonstrative was *þȳ* or *þē* for all genders, M.E. and N.E. *the*. *The*, in its instrumental function, before adjectives or adverbs in the comparative degree, is an adverb and not a definite article. Its use dates back to K. Alfred's *Boethius*. It is employed in English to the present day, e.g. '*the* sooner *the* better', its original meaning being 'by that'. Only one type of the usage, *the rather*, which is now obsolete, is here recorded. Its employment may be either temporal (meaning 'the sooner') or causal (meaning 'the more readily').

C.A. II. 1. 60 (126) he would resolve indeede/None were at home, and so breake in *the rather*

E.M.I.H. II. 1. 10 (220) I knowing of this conspiracie, and *the rather* to insinuate with my young master . . . have got me afore in this disguise

E.M.O.H. V. 2. 17 (567) He doth stay *the rather* . . . to present your acute iudgement with so courtly . . . a gentleman

Revels V. 10. 35 (172) It will tarry *the rather*, for the antiperistasis will keepe it in.

(*b*) There is an example in *Sejanus* of the omission of instrumental *the*, before the comparative *more*, for the sake of metre. This is a poetic licence and is uncommon.

Sej. II. 26 (376) Though I have lov'd you long, and with that height/Of Zeale, and dutie, (like the fire, which₍ₐ₎ more/It mounts, it trembles)

95. Occasional omission of 'the' in titles of office

This matter is discussed in Christophersen's *The Article*, § 74. Titles containing an *of*-phrase, he says, sometimes take the definite article and sometimes do not; with *real* titles, e.g. *the House of Lords* and *Edward Prince of Wales* it is regularly omitted The return of *the* in the modern title *Justice of the Peace* is therefore peculiar. Jonson has the title without definite article.

E.M.O.H. I. 2. 15 (444) I might be a Justice of₍ₐ₎ Peace (prose)

96. Omission of 'the' before 'other'

The use of *other* (without definite article) after *each, either, neither, one* and *none* in reciprocal constructions is very old, e.g. c. 893 K. Alfred *Oros.* II. 3 § 2 Heora þǣr ǣჳðer ōðerne ofslōg.

In L.M.E. the use of the definite article before *other* became frequent, probably being traceable to the 14th C reciprocal combination *on þe oper* (later *one another*). Constructions with and without the definite article were found side by side until the mid-17th C, when *the* was regularly required, except in the phrase *each other*, which remained as a relict of the old construction (see under Reciprocal Pronouns, § 81).

Jonson uses the old construction occasionally.

C.A. III. 3. 15 (150) I could have wisht some happier accident/Had made the way unto this mutuall knowledge,/Which either of us now must take of$_\wedge$ other,

E.M.I.H. I. 4. 213 (219) Sends like contagion to the memorie,/Still each of$_\wedge$ other catching the infection

97. Omission of 'the' after prepositions in adverbial phrases, chiefly of place.

Omissions of the definite article in adverbial phrases seem to be made by Jonson mainly for the sake of metre. They are common in 16th and 17th century poetry, and survive in some modern phrases, such as *at college, at home, in town*.

C.A. II. 1. 63 (126) and talke alowd,/As if there were some more in$_\wedge$ house with thee

Stap. N. II. 5. 124 (322) the blessed/Pokahontas (as the Historian calls her)/ . . . /Hath bin in$_\wedge$ womb of a taverne

Shakespeare, however, has several similar examples in prose: e.g. *Wint. Tale* IV 4. 700 Pray heartily he be at$_\wedge$ palace.

6. BIBLIOGRAPHY

TEXT

HERFORD AND SIMPSON, *Ben Jonson*, 11 vols., Clarendon Press,
1925-51

DICTIONARIES

New English Dictionary, Clarendon Press, 1933
BOSWORTH AND TOLLER, *Dictionary of Anglo-Saxon*, Clarendon
Press, 1898, Supplement, 1921
STRATMANN AND BRADLEY, *Middle English Dictionary*, O.U.P.,
1891
WRIGHT, *Dialect Dictionary*, O.U.P., 1898
SCHMIDT, *Shakespeare Lexicon*, Williams and Norgate, 1874
ONIONS, *Shakespeare Glossary*, Clarendon Press, 2nd ed., 1919
FOWLER, *Dictionary of Modern English Usage*, O.U.P., 1926

GRAMMARS

WRIGHT, *Old English Grammar*, O.U.P., 3rd ed., 1925
WRIGHT, *Elementary Middle English Grammar*, O.U.P., 2nd
ed., 1928
WRIGHT, *Elementary Historical New English Grammar*, O.U.P.,
1924
WRIGHT, *English Dialect Grammar*, O.U.P., 1905
SWEET, *A New English Grammar*, 2 parts; Clarendon Press,
1892 and 1898
GILL, *Logonomia Anglica* (1621), ed. O. L. Jiriczek, Trübner,
1903
BUTLER, *English Grammar* (1634), ed. A. Eichler, Max Nie-
meyer, Halle, 1910
DAINES, *Orthoepia Anglicana* (1640), ed. M. M. Rösler and
R. Brotanek, Halle, 1908
COOPER, *Grammatica Anglicana* (1685), ed. J. D. Jones, Max
Niemeyer, Halle, 1911
ABBOTT, *A Shakespearian Grammar*, Macmillan, 1879
FRANZ, *Shakespeare-Grammatik*, Max Niemeyer, Halle, 1939
MAETZNER, *English Grammar*, 3 vols, Murray, 1874
POUTSMA, *Grammar of Late Modern English*, 2nd ed., 5 vols.,
Noordhoff, 1928

KRUISINGA, *Handbook of Present-day English*, 4 vols., Groningen,-Noordhoff, 1931

JESPERSEN, *The Philosophy of Grammar*, Allen and Unwin, 1924

JESPERSEN, *Modern English Grammar*, 6 parts, Allen & Unwin, 1933-46

JESPERSEN, *Essentials of English Grammar*, Allen & Unwin 1933

JESPERSEN, *System of Grammar*, Allen & Unwin, 1933

CURME AND KURATH, *Grammar of the English Language*, 3 vols., Heath & Co., 1931

HISTORIES OF ENGLISH LANGUAGE

PEGGE, *Anecdotes of the English Language*, 2nd ed., Nichols & Bentley, 1814

STORM, *Englische Philologie*, Heilbronn, 1881

KELLNER, *Historical Outlines of English Syntax*, Macmillan, 1892

MORRIS, *Historical Outlines of English Accidence*, Macmillan, 1903

MOORE, *Tudor-Stuart Views on the Growth, Status and Destiny of the English Language*, Max Niemeyer, Halle, 1910

WYLD, *Short History of English*, Murray, 1921

WYLD, *History of Modern Colloquial English*, Blackwell, 1936

BRADLEY, *Making of English*, Macmillan, 1937

MATTHEWS, *Cockney Past and Present*, Routledge, 1938

JESPERSEN, *Growth and Structure of the English Language*, 7th ed., Blackwell, 1933

McKNIGHT, *Modern English in the Making*, Appleton-Century, 1928

BAUGH, *History of the English Language*, Appleton-Century, 1935

BOGHOLM, *English Speech from an Historical Point of View*, Allen & Unwin, 1939

MONOGRAPHS AND SPECIAL STUDIES

SCHRADER, *Das Altenenglische Relativpronomen*, Kiel, 1880

JESPERSEN, *Progress in Language*, Allen & Unwin, 1909

LANGENFELT, *Select Studies in Colloquial English of the Late Middle Ages*, Lund, 1933

DAHL, *Form and Function* (Studies in Old and Middle English Syntax), Copenhagen, 1936

DEN BREEJEN, *The Genitive and its Of- Equivalent in the latter half of the Sixteenth Century*, Amsterdam, 1937

CHRISTOPHERSEN, *The Articles*, O.U.P., 1939

VAN DE MEER, *Main Facts concerning the Syntax of Mandeville's Travels*, Utrecht, 1929

DEKKER, *Some Facts concerning the Syntax of Malory's Morte D'Arthur*, Amsterdam, 1932

ANDREW, *Syntax and Style in Old English*, C.U.P., 1940

ENGBLOM, *On the Origin and Development of the Auxiliary 'Do'*, Lund, 1938

JOURNALS

Anglia, vol. 3, O. Lohmann, 'Ueber die Auslassung des Englischen Relativ-pronomens, p. 115

Anglia, vols. 13 and 14, E. Einenkel, 'Die Quelle der Englischen Relativ-Elipse', vol. 13, p. 348; vol. 14, p. 122

Anglia, vol. 26, B.A.P. van Dam and C. Stoffel, 'The authority of the Ben Jonson Folio of 1616', p. 377

Anglia, vol. 26, E. Einenkel, 'Das Englische Indefinitum', p. 461

Anglia, vol. 36, P. Fyn van Draat, 'Rhythm in English Prose', pp. 1 and 493

Englische Studien, vol. 11, W. Franz, *Die Dialektsprache bei Ch. Dickens*, p. 197

Englische Studien, vol. 17, W. Franz, *Zur Syntax des Alteren Neuenglisch*, III possessiv pronomina, p. 384

Englische Studien, vol. 54, W. Franz, *Die Umschreibung mit 'do' in Shakespeares Prosa*

INDEX

103